MILLENNIAL MILLIONAIRE

MILLENNIAL MILLIONAIRE

*The Young Entrepreneur's Guide to
Breaking Out of the Middle Class*

MIKE ANDES

ISBN-13: 9780692743034
ISBN-10: 0692743030

TABLE OF CONTENTS

INTRODUCTION

"Sacrifice or regret...you choose."

CAMILO VILLEGAS

What if I told you the American middle class is vanishing? That our economy is changing at lightning speed and the tale of the American Dream that we have been sold on is nothing more than a lie? Today, Millennials are more likely than any other generation to examine and reject the "conveyor-belt" method of thinking—graduate high school, amass college debt, accumulate mortgage debt, and work 9–5 in a stable but unfulfilling job. As the most educated generation in American history, with student loan debt to prove it, more and more Millennials are arming themselves with the knowledge to break away from our nation's default setting of working themselves to the bone in hopes of achieving middle class status, the pillar of the American Dream.

If you are ready to break free from the middle class mindset, I want to help you cultivate an entrepreneurial mentality, reach your biggest goals, and live out your passions every day. Whether you are ready to exit the 9–5 routine, seek a new, rewarding career, or build your wealth through smart investments (which will allow you to focus on your true passions), get ready to learn concrete strategies for making these goals a reality.

This book examines the actions necessary for developing an entrepreneurial mindset, making the right investments and working smarter, not harder. Let me help you make intelligent decisions about homeownership, personal finance, and using college as an investment strategy rather than a societal expectation one must fulfill.

The Millennial Millionaire is a personal journey that rounds up the tools, techniques, and lessons I have learned on my path to becoming a successful entrepreneur, one who has built several prosperous businesses and a top-rated business podcast before the age of 20. Building the lifestyle I wanted through entrepreneurial endeavors was not an easy road, and I began at the same place you are right now—the beginning of the journey. I have made the mistakes and learned what works versus what does not and I am willing to share all of this information. By employing the correct mindset and combining it with the right tools, it is my belief Millennials are currently situated in an ideal position to earn the title of the most successful generation ever seen in history.

In 2008, at the age of 13, I began my first year of college. My parents and grandparents on both sides had never attended college, and with me being so young, there was an expectation to become the academic in the family. Our family had never been wealthy; in fact, we barely fit the income brackets necessary to be considered middle class. Hopes were held high for me to break the mold. With no abundance in money or freedom as far as finances were concerned, becoming middle class was something to aspire toward.

I was on this assumed road, one dreaded by so many Millennials; graduate with student loan debt, buy a house, get a mortgage, purchase a couple of cars, have a two-car garage, work 40 years in my trained industry, retire, and hope by some miracle that Social Security still existed.

However, like many young men and women, I questioned this so-called "American Dream" as I watched my parents and grandparents struggle and spend their days unfulfilled but bound by the purchases and obligations set forth by middle class expectations. Today, our generation is beginning to question this "safe route" —the conveyor-belt path comprised of going to college, working, and waiting for retirement to finally begin living. The 9–5 grind has definitely come in to question as well. There is no better time than the present to question our desires, passions, and life goals and determine if the assumed path to the "American Dream" lines up with our objectives or takes us off course. We have to start thinking about ways to take freedom into our own hands and not depend on the government for Social Security, benefits, healthcare, etc.

Entrepreneurship is the ticket out of all of this.

A WAKEUP CALL

In 2008, like so many people in America, my family and friends were severely affected by the housing bubble. It seemed almost everyone had bought into the idea of zero percent mortgages and flipping houses, even though their credit was not the best and they did not earn the income necessary to cover expenses. People were taking on huge amounts of risks, over-leveraging themselves and buying a house, because at some point they had been told home ownership is something to aspire to, something that makes you "American." Owning a home has been and still is weaved into the fabric of our country and the middle class mentality.

That was the year everything crashed and my family had to sell our dream home. All the gains made from 2005-2007 evaporated. I believe 2008 was a wakeup call for me and many of my fellow Millennials. When I use the term Millennials, I am referencing someone born between 1980 and 2000, according to the original term coined by Neil Howe and William Strauss. Back to 2008, that year is partly responsible for our generation's current disinterest in investing in the housing economy, purchasing homes, and investing in the stock market. The crash shook our belief that real estate was always going to go up in value. And after seeing our parents and grandparents lose their homes and retirement, we began to question everything we had been told that was supposedly financially wise or safe.

The idealistic American lifestyle, this middle class dream, was not as secure as we previously thought. The crash came down hard on the everyday person, especially those in the middle class. During this time, a lot of people began to recognize that many of the things our parents or politicians had communicated to us regarding what it was to be American, to be financially free, stable, and independent, had to be more closely examined. Millennials were finally beginning to see the middle class and the American Dream for what it truly is—a lifestyle that does not provide financial freedom and does not foster entrepreneurship.

YOUR USP

Shortly before 2008, as I was preparing to head to college and beginning to see the widespread effects the housing situation was having on my family, I knew there were no funds to pay for tuition. I also knew

I did not want to graduate with a mountain of debt that would take me years to repay. And so, using the entrepreneurial bug that I always seemed to possess, I created a lawn care business with my brother to help pay our college tuition costs.

A question that comes up repeatedly on my podcast is how can someone so young be taken seriously if they want to start a business. I see youth as a huge advantage when it comes to business and I advise Millennials to use it as their "unique selling proposition," or USP. As someone who loves marketing and advertising, I knew my brother and I had to use the fact that we were young as an advantage over other companies. There were countless lawn care businesses in our city, so how were we going to stick out? What was going to make us different?

Our marketing campaign revolved around the fact that we were young kids, 11 and 13, who were saving up for college. We were not old enough to drive and would literally be pushing mowers around our city and county, but believed we could catch a potential customer's attention by our USP—two young brothers who were willing to work hard in order to better themselves through college.

And so, we created these little flyers on Microsoft Publisher and worked on getting a list of names and addresses of people in our neighborhood. We had printed out 300 flyers, placed them in envelopes, and wrote everyone's information by hand. I still remember the day we took this massive box of envelopes and flyers to the post office, having been driven there by our father. We took them out, prayed over them, and hoped we would get some business.

Even today, we do not get the response rate that we received from that initial mailing. We took on many clients, 30 within the first couple of weeks, which is good in our industry. Augusta Lawn Care Services was not birthed by a lot of money. It began with a junky push mower that we ended up taking back three times before finally purchasing a Honda. In our first year, we made just over $3,000. For an 11 and 13-year-old, we truly believed we struck it rich! The next year we made $15,000 and the following year just over $30,000. Our business grew every year and essentially, we were able to pay for college and accumulate zero student loan debt. It just goes to show that something that seems like a weakness, for instance youth, can actually become a strength because it makes you unique.

PARADIGM SHIFT

While our lawn care business continued to excel, I spent four years in college preparing to enter medical school at the age of 17. As part of my capstone project for my Bachelor's degree at Western Washington University, I traveled to Kenya to experience medical care outside of the United States. Looking back, I can see being an entrepreneur was embedded in my thought process from a young age. Going to college and seeing what our educational system was all about, and then getting a reality check on the healthcare system while in Africa and the amount of poverty there, my thought process began to radically change.

Africa was a time for me to reflect not only on the comparisons in the medical field, but also on my future and what I truly wanted. I had to contemplate if I wanted to be a cog in this massive healthcare system and in the same specialty for the next 40 years of my life. Did I really want to put my future at risk by going into debt for medical school? The applications had been sent, the recommendation letters received. I was all set to begin medical school, but Africa brought about a season of deliberation.

I was not going into medicine for the money, and I knew I did not want to be tied to a medical office for the rest of my life. What I did want was a lifestyle that would offer me freedom, time to travel, and the ability to pursue philanthropic endeavors. I sincerely believed if I went into the medical field that I would become, for lack of a better word, a slave to the career, forced to lump my life's passions into one category. With entrepreneurship, I knew I would be able to diversify and do things I enjoy, such as running four or five different businesses at one time. While I am still passionate about health, medical research, and healthcare, today my entrepreneurship goals align with this industry in a different way than originally planned and offer me the freedom and security I desire.

If there is one thing I remember about the housing bubble and its fallout, it is the fear. When people are afraid, they act irrationally and make poor decisions. They say things they do not necessarily mean. I saw it happen in my own family and with close friends. The crash made me realize that I never wanted money to be a determining factor in the relationships I built. I have seen the anxiety and fear that comes along with not being able to pay bills. However, for those who have essentially made money their slave and not their master, whether or not they have any money does not put pressure on their relationship with their wife, husband, family, loved ones, etc.

Too many people make money their master. These are the people who are sacrificing many aspects of their life to make their business bigger, to earn more and more money. They are struggling and they have to go to work every day because if they do not, they will not be able to pay the bills that week. Those in a low to middle class standing who make money their master are similar to a millionaire who is spending a 100 hours a weeks away from his or her family, deserting their relationships and the things that are important in life. They are chained and bound and missing out on the enjoyment life can offer. This stress and fear was taking place in the relationships around me and I knew at that moment that I never wanted this to happen in my own life.

I took a second trip to Africa one year later, this time to Malawi. Africa has a special place in my heart and I set a goal to help build an orphanage in Kenya. While heading back from my second trip, my life goals had suddenly become much bigger. I knew a certain amount of money and freedom would be needed to achieve some of the goals I had already put into place, such as the orphanage. I made the decision to completely step away from medical school and I started my MBA, knowing business was the road I was meant to be traveling.

Since that trip, Augusta Lawn Care has seen 800 percent growth. I also co-founded BioShakes, a gym-based vending machine brand that delivers high-quality protein shakes on demand, and I created the Business Bootcamp podcast. The podcast has taken off because there are so many people, even outside of the Millennial generation, who want to learn more about investments, starting a business, and breaking free of the typical 9–5 lifestyle.

I tell my listeners if they can learn to live on little, it is going to serve them well in the future. When they have an idea or a goal they want to make happen in the future, it is so much easier to pursue because they have more budget to work with. The idea of running personal finances like a business is discussed often on the show. People need to know their financial numbers. Many are unaware of these figures. What is your breakeven? What is your profit margin? All of these concepts that are used in business finance can be applied directly to personal finance. How much money do you need to make every month to get by? I tell listeners if they can come up with that figure, they can begin working on lowering it, essentially increasing their profit margins.

The podcast also gets Millennials thinking about their goals or questioning goals that may have been influenced by family or societal expectations. Many are questioning whether the American Dream is something they really want to sacrifice their day for. Countless callers express their dislike for their job, or want to start a new business but cannot because of debt. There is a collective frustration in the typical middle class lifestyle and people are beginning to realize they want their independence back. They want to live out their passion and be financially free.

In the end, I ask them if they are chasing their own dreams or someone else's dreams.

I also ask if their dreams are being achieved by going to work for their employer.

More and more Millennials are questioning whether or not their current path is worth sacrificing a third of their day or a third of their life for something they are not passionate about. For those on the fence, I am here to remind you that control is in your own hands and you have the power to create your own financial freedom.

Action Steps and Reflection

As your read through this book, examine and evaluate your USP and determine how it can make your brand, business, or passion stand apart from the rest.

PART 1: THE MIDDLE CLASS NIGHTMARE

Chapter 1

● ● ●

THE DYING DREAM

LESS MEAT, MORE BUN

The security of the middle class is failing. According to a 2015 Pew Research Center analysis, the American middle class, which has served as the economic majority over the past 40 years, is now identical in number to the income tiers above and below it. To dig deeper into the economic changes of the middle class, we need to first identify it. In 2014, the Pew Research Center, using data from the U.S. Census Bureau and the Federal Reserve Board of Governors, defined the middle class as those whose annual household income is approximately $42,000 to $126,000 for a household of three. If we calculated annual incomes for the U.S. population using this definition, we would wind up with a figure of 50 percent of the adult population landing in the middle class income tier bracket for 2015. Compare this to 61 percent of the population in 1971 and you can see a polarization of classes beginning to take place.

Income however is not the only determining factor in the "middle class" definition. In 2010, the U.S. Department of Commerce released a report titled *Middle Class in America* that discusses how the aspirations of an individual can also identify them as middle class. For example, the report defined middle class as a "combination of values, expectations, and aspirations, as well as income levels." The report found those who are aspiring to be part of the middle class desire economic stability, a home, secure retirement, the ownership of vehicles, family vacations, and the ability to send their children to college.

A February 2015 Pew Research Center survey also shared that nine out of 10 people who consider themselves middle class determine this label not only by their earnings and assets but also by their aspirations. Study after study shows the desire of most people to achieve middle class status. However, this middle class dream that was once depicted as a lifestyle that provides stability, optimism, and contentment is now being shrouded by anxiety, stress, and discontentment. Why is this? For starters, it is a combination of the instability in incomes, unpredictable job prospects, being vulnerable to economic tides, etc.

Let's use the vulnerability aspect as an example. People in the middle class income bracket are going to be more vulnerable to the economic tides, whether it is the stock market, housing market, job market, etc. Say someone is making $90,000 and they adopt this middle class mentality, this American Dream theology. They bought two cars, or worse, leased them, and they have a big mortgage and many types of expenses. When it is all averaged out, this individual's savings at the end of the day is such an insignificant amount of his or her annual income that there is barely any money for retirement or to have financial freedom.

When I use the term *freedom*, I am speaking about having a certain level of peace in knowing if something went wrong financially, say someone was in an accident, there was a fire in the home, or another type of calamity transpired, they would financially be able to stay afloat. To get a better understanding of typical savings for someone in the middle class, let's borrow data from the U.S. Department of

Commerce's January 2010 report titled <u>Middle Class in America</u>. In one section of this report, a graph details a hypothetical budget for a married couple with two school-aged children. This "couple" is earning $122,800 annually— landing them in a top tier income bracket within the middle class. Even at this income level, the couple's typical annual savings for retirement is $4,100, just 3.3 percent according to the report. Whether they are truly using this "savings" for retirement or for a rainy day, $4,100 will not get them very far should a disaster strike.

Many people who consider themselves to be middle class are living right on the same edge as the couple highlighted in the report mentioned. It would literally take one thing going wrong—a job loss, a housing market crash, an illness—and they could be living in poverty. The reality is, the middle class is vulnerable from many different angles. This is why you are seeing so many people going up or down in terms of their income bracket status to lower or upper class. People are fed up with feeling vulnerable, insecure, and unable to get ahead. They are either working their way out of the middle class by creating their own business, getting a second job, or downsizing their home in order to rise above it or they are going downward.

Those who choose to go downward will stay in the $20,000 - $40,000 income range, will not have to pay as many taxes, may get food stamps and government assistance, and will never be financially free. If you are wondering why someone would willingly choose to step downward, it is actually an easier lifestyle because they are not being crushed from as many angles as someone in the middle class. And as more and more people move from the middle class to the lower and upper classes, we will see a polarizing of the rich and poor. The purpose of my Business Bootcamp podcast and of this book is to push people with big goals and ambitions to head in a positive direction rather than going downhill.

A NOT-SO-JUICY BURGER

Let's say you walk into your favorite burger joint, specifically a fast food restaurant. On the menu, you see this incredible photograph of a burger. There is a massive patty that gives off an appearance of five pounds of beef, an awesome looking patty, and some lettuce, tomato, and cheese. Then you receive your order and there is a large bun and this tiny piece of meat somewhere in there. This is the image I see when thinking about the middle class.

People are drooling over this menu item that has been completely Photoshopped to be extremely appealing. The exact same thing is happening with the American Dream—it looks like there is so much meat, so much freedom, and complete independence—but when you achieve it, it is all bun. There is no sustenance. It will not fill you up. It will not satisfy you and it most definitely will not allow you to fulfill your goals.

This burger also serves as a representation of how the middle class is getting smaller, while the "bun" on both sides is getting larger—the rich are increasing their wealth and poverty is on the rise. In fact, a 2014 study from the U.S. Census Bureau titled *Income, Poverty, and Health Insurance Coverage in the United States* stated that 15 percent of people in America were living in poverty, 2.3 percent more than just before the 2008 recession.

At the end of the day, the American Dream is nothing more than a Photoshopped image that our politicians and society have fed us over many years, yet millions of people are not fulfilled. And while this impeccable image is still being served on the menu, I believe many Millennials are looking for somewhere else to dine.

EDUCATION AND THE MIDDLE CLASS

About 70 percent of my Business Bootcamp podcast callers are Millennials. For the most part, they are questioning the assumed road ahead of them, especially when it comes to college versus starting a business. In the past, if you were to go to college and graduate with a degree, you set yourself apart from everyone else. It was your USP going back 30 to 40 years ago. Back then, you would graduate, find a job, and have a distinct advantage as compared to a large portion of the population. Nowadays, with financial aid, grants, scholarships, and FAFSA, attending college has become a much more level playing field and earning a degree does not set you apart.

When our parents or grandparents graduated from college, they could rely on that degree to help them find a job, earn a good living, and propel them into a middle class lifestyle. They were able to offer their family financial security and even receive a pension in many cases when it came time to retire. Today, Millennials are watching classmates graduate college after many years of studying only to struggle to find a position in the field they studied. They are also watching their generation be overwhelmed by student debt into their mid-to-late 30s and 40s. Many were sold on the illusion that higher education would offer them freedom and yet this combination of debt and the inability to find employment is stifling their dreams and hindering them from achieving their goals.

Today we have engineering graduates flipping burgers whereas 40 or 50 years ago this degree would have almost always guaranteed an incredible career. And it is not only happening here in America. When I visited Africa, I spoke with some of the drivers of Matatus (small buses that carry up to 25 passengers). I learned through these conversations that several had graduated with their Master's degrees yet could not find a position in the field in which they were trained. While Africa may be a total different ballgame in terms of economics as compared to America, it just goes to show you in today's world, education is not a ticket into financial freedom. I believe entrepreneurship is the path many are seeking.

When discussing entrepreneurship, I am not only speaking about wanting to start a business. The mindset also encompasses taking responsibility for your life and setting big goals. Today, I believe more and more workplaces and corporations are beginning to see the value in potential employees who possess this mindset. Companies such as Google, Apple, and Microsoft, all of which encourage entrepreneurial ideals and pursuits, are setting the stage. These companies have come to the realization that an entrepreneur's ideals can propel a corporation forward. They understand fostering this type of mindset is going to help their company create great, new products and services. Entrepreneurs working within these types of corporations are becoming known as "intrapreneurs," and they are running their corporate position like a business. These men and women can easily engage with others, build connections, create new ideas and bring them to fruition, all while managing a team and having great communication skills. I think Millennials, whether they are creating their own business or acting an as intrapreneur at a corporation, must possess these qualities in order to be set apart.

AVERAGE IS NOT GOOD ENOUGH

Think about the transition from middle school to high school. Everyone is trying to fit in, trying to be average. It is around this time many people set average goals, average ambitions, and average dreams for themselves. The reason people get trapped in the middle class is because their goals brought them there. It is not because they were unlucky or did not work hard enough—in most cases it is due to their goals being outdated middle class ones.

Have you ever heard a child say, "I want to be an astronaut," or "I want to be a billionaire," and the next statement made is a parent or teacher telling the child to be realistic or choose something everyone else is doing? Well, what is "realistic?" In essence, what they are saying is, "Think average. Think like everyone else."

This type of mindset does not foster creativity or push young men and women to create innovative solutions to any of the problems we have in our society or economy. Now is the time to encourage people to think outside of the box; to support those who are willing to put an abnormal amount of energy and time into an idea they have, into their goals, in order to make their larger-than-average ambitions a reality. That is really where it all begins—goal setting. Go for what you want in life. Have big goals and break out of the mentality that has been placed on us to follow certain rules and take a prescribed track in life. Remember, average will not give you the freedom and stability you are seeking.

THE VALUE OF GOALS

I do not discuss the topic of entrepreneurship on my Business Bootcamp podcast in order to only teach people how to make money. The goal is to help listeners achieve the freedom in life that allows them to do the things they truly value. Your goals are what drive you to make money. For example, during one of my trips to Africa I met a woman named Margaret. She had taken 70 orphans into her three-bedroom, two-bathroom home. In addition to schooling and feeding these children, she was entirely responsible for all of their needs. No government funding was coming her way. My dream, or one of them, is to build a new orphanage for these children. This is a big goal that will require a lot of money. The businesses I am building with BioShakes and Augusta Lawn Care Services are not to make money only for the sake of accumulating a greater balance in my bank account—they are to help me reach my larger goals.

If I met someone who had goals that did not require a lot of money, I would advise them to *not* spend 100 hours a week working on a business, to go do something they would enjoy. Do something that is aligned with your goals, whatever your passion is, because spending a lot of time on something you do not enjoy is just wasting your life. Having money for the sake of having it is not something to strive for. Finding out what your goals are *is* something to strive for.

If your goals are big and require a lot of funding, then you will have to sacrifice a lot of time and energy. There is going to have to be a business, a job, or some sort of investment involved to reach your goal. Determine what your goals are and line them up to what you are currently doing. If your current path is not aligned with your goals, then it is time to make a change. You only get one life to live out your dreams.

Chapter 2

● ● ●

THE MIDDLE CLASS MANTRA

When I was 13, I had to meet with a program advisor and the president of the community college I was about to attend. Because I was soon to be the youngest student ever at the college, the meeting was more of an assessment of my maturity rather than an interview. At the time, I had a consuming desire to be a heart surgeon. We began working on my class plan and I could not wait to take sciences classes, nutrition, and technology courses and anything else that focused on the human body. Unfortunately, I kept being directed into a liberal arts workload, with random electives that were supposedly going to make me more "well-rounded." This urging to steer more in the direction of a liberal arts education rather than study a field that was a passion of mine was a let down.

Why are college students pushed into this mindset of becoming well-rounded? If everyone is receiving this well-rounded education, we suddenly all become average and fit in with everyone else. We have no distinct advantage over workplace competition. What is wrong with a student having a goal and relentlessly going after it? While the program advisor had tried to push me to accept reasonable education goals, I refused to follow suit and was eventually allowed to study pre-medicine courses.

To some degree, people like to stand out. Maybe it is their hair or their fashion choices, but we do not see this behavior as much in Millennials when it comes to education. Once many of them are attending high school; they are already planning the road that will get them to a job that pays $70,000 a year, enables them to buy a few cars, a house, and perhaps take a vacation each year. Why not? Everyone else is doing it. In general, people follow along with this mindset because teachers, counselors, and parents continually encourage it as they are growing up. People begin adopting this herd mentality, sticking together and doing the same thing.

While some Millennials do like to stick out, for the most part many of us compare ourselves to those around us. We compare ourselves to what is thought of as "successful" and then we plan our goals around it. Think about this in terms of testing. When you are in high school and receive a test score back, the teachers do not focus so much on how many students received a 100 percent on the quiz. They focus on the class average. You see the same thing on SAT scores and standardized tests—again, you are compared to the average. It is because we are constantly programmed to think of average as the place you want to be and what you want to strive for.

PREDATOR VS. PREY

The mindset of fitting into the crowd reminds me of a predator versus prey survival technique. Let's say a lion is hunting an antelope. The lion will go for the antelope that sticks out or looks different in some way. A survival tactic for this antelope is to stick close to the others and become part of the crowd. A group of antelopes will stick close to one another to look larger, so they all fit in, look the same, and do not get attacked. I think when it comes to education and work, people take on this herd mentality and assume if you fit in with the rest of the crowd and become averagely successful, you will not be attacked or questioned.

The problem with this is in today's world, trying to hide or fit in with everyone else will not work when it comes down to whether or not you will face your fears and try to achieve your dreams. The predator versus prey becomes a one-on-one battle rather than a group battle. Every person will have to decide for him or herself whether they are going to become part of the middle class or put in large amounts of work, go after their dreams, and propel upward.

If we keep comparing ourselves to the average, we limit ourselves. People have the capability of moving so far beyond the ordinary, but because we are constantly compared to middle class expectations and the status quo, we are falling short of our true potential. Bottom line: When people are ready to get out of the middle class mindset, they realize they need to let go of the herd mentality and stop shooting for average.

THE FALLACY OF REASONABLE GOALS

Fifty to 100 years ago, it worked for many people to have reasonable goals in life. It worked to have an education, get a house, and follow the "safe route." Even if someone was working in a field they did not love, they did it because it provided for their family and they knew they would have a retirement and be supported by the government. Now, this safe route is being questioned. Following the safe route today can mean you are working in a field you dislike, you are sacrificing a large portion of your time for something that does not offer you enough money to pay off your home, have a retirement plan, or even have job security.

Decades ago, you could expect to work at a company for 40 years and then rely on the government for retirement. Today, this is not a reality. If someone tried to apply the same education and work strategies that were used in the past to today's reality, they will either fall into the middle class and live an average life at best or will not be able to find a job and eventually life will fall apart. Today there is always someone to replace you at your job. And people cannot assume Social Security will be around to help them in their retirement.

Even for people outside of the Millennial generation, the security of retirement is slipping through their hands. According to a 2015 report from the National Institute on Retirement Security, nearly 45 percent of working-age households do not own any retirement account assets. In addition, the average working household has literally no retirement savings, with a typical savings of just $2,500.

When it comes to relying on government systems, I encourage podcast callers to forget about Social Security in terms of retirement. The system is broke, inefficient, and most likely will not exist when Millennials reach their 60s, 70s, 80s, and so on. The message to this generation is to put matters of your financial future and retirement into your own hands and don't expect to be able to rely on the government.

During the crash, the government bailed out a lot of people and countless companies. The deficit is only increasing and eventually there has to be a breaking point. Whether they cut Social Security, Medicaid, or funding for veterans, we need to get out of the mindset that our retirement is secure through government support.

Reasonable, average goals are no longer working in today's society. Your goals need to be greater than just existing at a job you do not like and that is not offering you any freedom. Your goals must include a plan for retirement and financial freedom.

If you continue aspiring to only reasonable goals, you will be vulnerable to the shifts in the economy, technology, the marketplace, and so many other areas that were not a threat 50 or 100 years ago. Lifestyle strategies that worked in the past are not working today, so our goals need to be overhauled and upgraded.

HOW TURMOIL CAN BE FRUITFUL

The economic turmoil we have seen since the housing market crash has actually been a good thing for Millennials. In the past couple of decades, many people in America have held on to old ideas, such as the ideas of the factory, assembly lines, people doing manual labor and grunt work, and just getting by. Because of the inability to let go of some of these ideas, we did not adapt fast enough to technology or the economic climate. And so, we have been left with a good amount of turmoil in many areas of life.

Essentially, the crash brought everything into doubt and spurred Millennials to start thinking differently. Millennials are finally seeing that what we did in the past is not working today and they are asking what can be done differently in order to get ahead. They see the answer in entrepreneurship and taking back the control we gave up in the past.

Now is the time to take control of your finances, healthcare, retirement, housing, etc. The conveyor-belt mentality is changing just like our technology and economic climate. Even the way the world does business is evolving and we need to adapt in order to be a part of it. It is time for Millennials to take control and reject the antiquated strategy of college, debt, working 9–5 for 40 years, and retiring on Social Security.

Since aspirations are so intimately connected to the definition of the middle class, a logical solution for Millennials to push themselves out of the middle class lifestyle and mindset would be to have higher aspirations. Aspirations are also connected to goal setting, which is the starting place for our generation to get themselves off the malfunctioning conveyor belt and into a world where they can live out their passions.

Action Steps and Reflection

Think back to your dreams as a child or teenager. Were those dreams diminished or have you continued to follow your original path?

Make a list of your top three goals and dreams without putting any limitations on yourself. What are some ways you can move closer to achieving them? Read over these goals regularly and research others who have accomplished similar feats. Envisioning success and seeing it can be done will help you keep your momentum.

Chapter 3

● ● ●

THE AMERICAN DREAM AND HOUSING

Is purchasing a house the financially prudent thing to do? It is a question I have asked and been asked countless times on my podcast. To better explain how I devise an answer for a given situation, let's take a step back for a moment.

In 2004, my family and friends became heavily involved in the real estate market. In the past, my family had always struggled with debt and many times hovered close to the poverty line. Then the Federal Reserve Board began slashing interest rates, and money to purchase a home suddenly became extremely easy to borrow. All of a sudden we were qualifying for zero percent down mortgages, building houses and over-leveraging ourselves…but everything was working out (or so we thought.)

We sold four spec homes, built two more, and began construction on my family's "dream home." Situated on five acres, with every area of the interior customized, it was everything we had ever dreamed. We were finally out of debt and vacationing, something we had never been able to do as a family. Just as we were wrapping up the building on our latest homes, the crash occurred and it happened quicker than we ever imagined. The spec homes we built had been selling for around $400,000 and within a few weeks were suddenly worth less than $300,000. We had taken on massive mortgages and loans at zero percent banking on the idea that we would pre-sell the house before construction was complete.

When the two spec homes were finished, just as the crash was occurring, we tried to get out of them as quickly as possible and still make a profit. We were unsuccessful. Now we were stuck with these two homes plus our dream home, completely over-leveraged and responsible for mortgages that would essentially require us being millionaires in order to pay off each month.

Our yearly income changed so drastically before the housing bubble and we had banked on the idea that each year our income and the housing market would continue to increase. We were just experiencing our first taste of "middle class living." Then suddenly, we were left with three homes that no one wanted to acquire unless the price was literally cut in half, and even then most people did not want to purchase anything.

Eventually we moved into one of the two spec homes and had to sell our dream home. We were right back to where we were before the housing bubble in terms of income and lifestyle. The second spec home ultimately sold and we stayed in the one spec home at a loss. Before the crash, I had witnessed for the first time ever my family reaching their financial dreams. We had achieved financial security only to see it ripped away because we had centered our financial future on something that was not stable. The experience left a taste in my mouth of what can happen when someone buys into the housing market when they are not financially qualified. I saw firsthand what materializes when you make decisions that hinge on a market always going up or based on the marketing ability of a politician or a bank telling you that it is an investment, a wise opportunity, and something that can improve your financial situation.

Not only did my family travel down this road, but I also witnessed numerous friends and family members experience a similar fate. It seemed everyone was going into foreclosure, filing for bankruptcy, or walking away from their homes completely. The experience radically changed my ideas about investing in the housing market and taught me numerous lessons that I now share with callers on the podcast.

TIED DOWN: BUYING INTO THE DREAM

One of the main ideals of the American Dream is homeownership. It is thought of as a good investment, a good way to build equity and lay a foundation for your family's financial future. A picture of the classic American family has been ingrained in all of us—a home, a mortgage, a two-car garage, and two purchased vehicles. Homeownership has become a large part of the middle class culture and is something celebrated when achieved. It is an indicator in our society that someone attained middle class status and the American Dream.

When someone does achieve the middle class goal of homeownership, are they truly getting the stability and freedom often portrayed in the American Dream? Often times, when thinking of homeownership, I feel it is something that can be binding, something that can tie you down to one geographical location. I have seen it bind people from better opportunities and keep them from achieving more in their life because they were tied to this massive liability. After the crash, I witnessed people staying in a home even if they had an opportunity somewhere else because they were underwater on their mortgage or they could not sell the house for their original purchase price.

I want to point out owning real estate is not bad; I am actually a huge proponent of it. In fact, I plan to purchase my own single-family residence in the near future. That being said, there are some negative aspects of home ownership some people do not take into consideration...especially Millennials. As Millennials, we need to be asking ourselves *why* we are buying a house, just as we should be asking ourselves why we are attending college. Is it solely because it is part of the American Dream and these ideologies have been passed down to us or is it because it is the financially prudent thing to do that will ultimately help us achieve our goals?

There was a call into my podcast that made the case of how home-ownership can actually be binding, especially to a Millennial. A listener from Oregon explained his situation of working in a 9–5 job and having a small business on the side. He received a job offer in Florida, working at another 9–5 that lined up more with his passions and paying triple his current salary. As much as he desperately wanted to take the position, he had a $3,500 per month mortgage and a single-family residence (SFR) that was not even worth two-thirds of what he origi-nally paid, as he had purchased it in the midst of the housing boom.

This scenario brought to my attention for the first time the real cost of owning a home; it revealed how during times when the housing market or economy is down, you can be tied to a piece of real estate if it is a large part of your net worth or the mortgage is a sizable por-tion of your income. While this caller had thought perhaps he could rent his home, he would only be able to charge $1,500 per month, leaving him $2,000 in the hole and basically eliminating the gains of moving away. This was the first call of many people who bought at the peak of the boom and were now reaping the negative effects because they were tied to a specific geographic location. This person could not chase a better opportunity that was right in front of him.

Part of the risk of owning a house is that if the value goes down and you are not able to sell it for the original purchase price, it could tie you to that physical location and keep you from chasing a job or other opportunity. The new position this caller was interested in was going to offer upward mobility and valuable experience that he had been craving. While he was deliberating what to do, the company hired someone else. I specifically remember him calling into the podcast several months later and expressing his disappointment in how the person this company had hired was now in a position he has chased after for so many years. Even though this caller was on the tail end age-wise of being a Millennial, he was still feeling the effect of making a decision based on a social norm and the expectation to purchase a home. Since that podcast episode some time ago, there have been countless callers who had an opportunity, an investment, or a job located somewhere else but were unable to chase it because they purchased a home that was far beyond their means. They were underwater with their mortgage, they could not sell their home, and they were not able to rent it without taking a substantial loss.

These situations are just one of the reasons why I am against Millennials purchasing an SFR as their first home. If someone is bent on purchasing an SFR, I remind him or her to determine whether they can cover their downsides. For instance, if better opportunities occur or say a family crisis strikes and they are forced to move away, is their downside covered—can they rent their house out for enough money that covers the mortgage at a minimum? I encourage people to watch their downsides because another 2008 will happen. Whether it occurs in five or ten years, our culture is cyclic, which is why you see recession, recovery, recession, recovery, and so on. Investment and multi-housing properties are a different story altogether from SFRs and we will examine their pros and cons in Chapter 8.

PREVENTING A REPEAT SCENARIO

Before the housing bubble, it did not make sense for a lot of people to get zero percent down mortgages and million dollar lines of credit when they were making $40,000 a year and had debt and no assets.

And yet, these mortgages were being handed out left and right. Some people felt it did not make sense and it was not sustainable, and then there was another group of people who were baited into making a poor decision. These people bought into the big banks and politicians who portrayed home buying at that time as something that would be a great investment long-term. These financial institutions and politicians were banking on people once again falling for the financially freeing and liberating act that is homeownership.

House prices were doubling each year and banks were pitching the idea that homeownership was the financially prudent thing to do; an investment in the future though millions were over-leveraging themselves. Even today, even with the aftermath of the housing bubble, many first-time homebuyers ask what is the maximum amount loan they can qualify for. They are seeking a nicer, bigger home in a better neighborhood and I think this mindset is completely backward. What these first time homebuyers should be determining is how much they can actually afford. They need to determine how much they can pay upfront, what they can pay each month, and if their downsides are covered or if they can rent the house to cover the mortgage should they have to relocate. Millennials and other people seeking out a home loan rarely examine many of these questions and figures.

While I do believe some people are more cautious today after witnessing the fallout of the housing market in 2008, homeownership is still a large part of the middle class culture, with many banks specifically glamorizing first time homeownership. And with the housing market having somewhat improved, banks and massive corporations are beginning to once again pitch to the America public that stability is back and homeownership is the way to go.

It is a great risk to allow our conceptions of finances and stability and our preconceived notions of society standards to dictate our financial decisions, decisions about our career, goals, etc. It is dangerous to allow the herd mentality to keep us from achieving our personal and financial goals. I think the 2008 housing bubble is a perfect example of what the American public and Millennials will need to change in terms of their mindset to ensure our future doesn't include repeating the past mistakes.

Action Steps and Reflection

Think of a few examples regarding people you know who were entangled in a messy home ownership situation, from being underwater with their mortgage to losing their home due to overleveraging themselves. What lessons can you learn from their experiences?

Chapter 4

● ● ●

THE AMERICAN DREAM AND EDUCATION

Going back 50 or 100 years ago, if someone had the opportunity to attend college, they had the opportunity to change their life (and potentially the life of their family). As an example, let's use a family of farmers who sends their son away to the city to attend college and ultimately become a physician or lawyer. Historically, education was always looked on as the ticket out of a mundane or poverty-stricken life. Decades ago, when someone got an education, they were setting themselves apart from others. In a way, they were unique and their college degree was the differentiating factor when they applied for a job.

Today, parents are still advising their children to attend college because it is a way into the middle class lifestyle. This mindset worked decades ago because percentage-wise, not that many people had a college degree. The more advanced your degree was, the more distinctive opportunities became available. That unique selling proposition, or USP, helped college graduates decades ago, but it's been diminished and almost eradicated by the fact that millions of people are now earning their college degree. Currently, when someone graduates with a Communications or Biology degree, no longer is that degree their USP. It cannot be because so many other people have also earned it. While a large percentage of Millennials have a degree (19 percent have already earned some type of degree according to a 2010 Pew Research study), we are learning that a degree alone is not the ticket to a good career, financial freedom, or a middle class lifestyle. More and more graduates are unemployed or underemployed and taking a job flipping burgers.

The ideology to push young adults to attend college in order to achieve a better life is still ingrained in our culture, but it is incorrect and has many flaws. Tuition costs are literally going through the roof, and state funding is declining. With this rise in tuition, I see a lot of people beginning to ask whether going to college and taking on substantial debt is worth it in the long run. People's eyes are opening to the fact that the educational system when it comes to colleges and universities is in fact a big business, and they want to know if their investment is going to pay any returns.

Many parents are not asking whether sending their child to college is the financially prudent thing to do because it is so ingrained in their mind that it is the "safe" thing to do—that college will set you up financially in the future and one just needs to sacrifice now in order to receive long-term benefits. The problem with this pattern of thinking is that so many people are getting educated today that having a college education is no longer a USP. When they graduate with a common degree and need to compete for a job with thousands of other men and women who have the same degree, how can they position themselves as unique in the job marketplace? The answer is, they cannot. And, because a degree is no longer setting anyone apart, it is time to start thinking about a new way to create your USP.

THE PRICE OF BEING BOUND

For Millennials who have attended college, many are now being crushed under the weight of student loan debt. An October 2015 *Wall*

Street Journal report shared 34 percent of Millennials, with an annual household income of $75,000 or higher, feel they will never be able to repay their student loans in full. Many are tapping into their retirement accounts in order to pay their monthly student loan debt.

Considering these figures are for Millennials who have been lucky enough to find decent paying jobs, you have to wonder how much trouble those without good-paying jobs are experiencing to pay off their student loan debt. Not only are good portions of Millennials being stressed out by the amount of student loan debt on their plates, but they are also being bound financially. It is putting them at risk if a calamity happens—they simply will not have enough money on hand. It will also bind them from chasing their dreams or a better opportunity, in addition to locking them into a job they may not like because they are completely dependent on a steady paycheck.

Time after time, I hear from Millennials on the podcast who are doing something they are not passionate about because they need the money to repay their student loans. A couple recently called in stating they had just paid back over $100,000 in student loan debt—they were both almost 40 years old. I wanted to know what they received their degrees in; he had been a political science major and she focused on communications, which are two degrees that are oversaturated in today's marketplace, making finding good job prospects difficult. Their scenario got my wheels spinning; I had to question what the outcome would have been if they had graduated high school, worked at a job, maybe working up to $15 an hour or so, and had just saved their money over these past 20 something years. Where would they have been today, financially speaking? Was getting a degree and amassing $100,000 in debt worth it in the end? It turned out he was making around $15 an hour, even with his degree, and he was now questioning whether spending the past 15 years being bound to this loan had been worth it as he had to put certain goals and dreams on hold.

From a financial and goal standpoint, pausing your goals and dreams until your massive student loan is repaid is not something a Millennials has to do today. As a Millennial, your early and mid-20s are one of the most productive and energy filled segments of your life. Many people are chasing financial independence during that period and are at the same time sacrificing some of the most important years of their life in college. While some are chasing an antiquated dream of sacrifice now in college and get rewarded later, many are realizing there is no job security or financial freedom in solely getting a college degree anymore. It is no longer a surefire ticket to the middle class, to making a good income, or to having any type of financial independence. College holds some people back from their goals, and not just during four or six years during college, but also because of the time they need to spend repaying their debt. A shift is beginning to take place and Millennials are questioning how they want to spend their most impactful and energetic years.

TINKERING WITH AN IDEA

One of those Millennials who began to question his career path was my close friend Johnathan, who had always obsessed with engineering. He loved solving things and eventually went to college for mechanical engineering. In his particular case, he did not go into a substantial amount of debt because he was able to work for his dad throughout college, which helped him financially. If someone loves engineering and has their mindset on being an engineer, my advice to them is to attend college. And so, Johnathan set out for a degree in engineering and eventually began working at the quintessential engineering job. Everyone in his circle wanted this cushy job, which paid good money and even had the perk of a company car.

We traveled to Europe together at one point and I remember during the last week of our trip, I could not wait to get home. I was about to acquire another company and, honestly, was itching to get back to work. Johnathan on the other hand, had a different feeling. He confided in me that he dreaded going to work and wished he never had to go back. I remembered not too long ago he had been sharing how amazing his position was and we all assumed he was exactly where he wanted to be, but something had drastically changed. A week later, he sent me a long text message explaining how unhappy he was with his life and how he did not feel challenged. Jonathan felt stuck in his job because the money was good and people would think there was something wrong with him if he walked away from this great opportunity. Then he asked me, "What should I do?"

The first thing I needed to determine was whether he just wanted to vent or if he wanted advice. While I had been asked this question many times on my podcast, this scenario was a bit different because I consider him a close friend. In all of the years we had known each other, I knew he was an entrepreneur at heart. His father had his own business and had achieved financial freedom. He saw me loving what I did for a living and how I had the freedom to make my own schedule and not worry about time. I think he knew all along he was an entrepreneur but it was finally time to admit it. "You have got to get aligned with what you really want out of life," I explained. I told Johnathan to consider three things—what he was good at, what he could be paid for, and what he loved to do. Being able to identify those three things and seeing where all three could align would be his answer to moving forward. We drew three circles and worked on these areas together, discussing what he was passionate about and what he loved doing.

In the end, being an inventor lined up with all three of these categories. He had some amazing ideas for creating a generator that tied into sustainable energy. We realized while this goal was achievable, he was going to need an extremely large amount of money to make it happen.

We discussed further what ideas he could pursue *now* that could begin generating income quicker, in order to help him achieve his financial goals while also doing work he enjoyed. He quickly came up with an incredible truck rack invention. His father made loading systems for trucks, so the supply chain from China was already in operation. The parts were all there; he just needed to make the decision to pursue his dream.

I remember seeing his eyes light up and ever since then he has been working nonstop on the idea and getting prepared to mass-market the product. Essentially, my friend has the inventing bug. He came to realize the education and the debt he accumulated was not in line with what he truly wanted in life, but it took him a while to accept this because he had put so much time and effort into getting a degree in order to land a job he did not enjoy.

Johnathan's story is a good reminder that down the road many of us may want to change careers. To invest the most crucial years of your life to earn a degree, which may limit you to one field or industry, in addition to the debt you will likely amass, may not be the most economically viable thing to do. This is why I did not choose to go into medicine. When contemplating spending 10 or 12 years going to school, getting a fellowship, and completing residency, I was not convinced that I wanted to be in that career for the rest of my life. Ten years is a long time, and you have to ask yourself what else can you be doing with all of this time? What experiences can you have? Could you be using these years in a different way in order to reach your goals quicker? I believe these are some of the questions Millennials need to be asking themselves when they are considering college and how they want to spend some of the most fruitful years of their life.

THREE CIRCLES

Sometimes when you do not follow your passions in life, you will be faced with disappointing consequences. There was a caller not too long ago on the podcast who was the perfect example of this situation. Michael had created a unique website that helped small business owners find the right employees—almost like a LinkedIn for small businesses. He had already created the algorithm and the website was about 80 percent complete. In addition to the website needing to be refined, he realized he needed money to kick off the website and marketing campaign, plus more of his time would have to be spent focusing specifically on this endeavor. He was at a crossroad, with his current employment steering him in one direction and this entrepreneurial endeavor in another. A decision needed to be made regarding whether or not he would make the jump, focus on this website and potentially not earn much money over the next year, or not pursue it at all. With a large amount of student loan debt weighing on him, Michael made the decision to wait a few more years and try to pay some of his student loan debt down. Within one year, a larger company knocked off his website and launched it into the marketplace. It took off.

This example once again shows going into debt for school and education can really bind someone from moving forward. One of this man's biggest goals—to build this website, take it public, and own his own business—had to be put on hold and eventually terminated and extinguished because he had held on to the idea that education was going to be his ticket to freedom. Now he is buried in debt.

Many Millennials find themselves in this position. Because of their student loan debt, they are putting off their goals for longer and longer periods. I have even spoken to some Millennials who do not want to get married until they have repaid their debt. Even on a social level, this debt is affecting their relationships and many other aspects of their life. These men and women are putting their goals, ambitions, and lives on hold at a time when they should be growing, expanding, and making good use of the energy they have.

It all comes back to those three circles I mentioned earlier. What are you good at? What are you passionate about? And what can you get paid for? I believe if people searched their souls and found the answers to these questions earlier in life, many would avoid going directly to college after high school. They would realize that getting a degree and going into debt is not directly aligned with their goals. They might realize they are only enrolling in college because it is what they have been told to do. It is what our parents, our teachers, and our high school counselors all push us to do. For many of these role models, they feel like they have done a good job or fulfilled their role if they can get us to enroll in college. Honestly, if students took a step back and determined what they wanted out of life, and narrowed down what they are really passionate about, we would see a lot of college students changing majors or putting off college altogether because they realize it is not going to get them any closer to where they want to be.

I want to quickly point out that I do not have a problem with education, but what I do have a problem with is people spending many years of their life and tens (or hundreds) of thousands of dollars on something that is not aligned with their end goal.

JUMPING OFF

Let's say you hate your current 9–5 job and you are in debt but you want to pursue your own business or idea. My first piece of advice is do not quit your day job, especially if you have a family, debt, and other obligations. This was also my first piece of advice to my engineer pal. I told him to stay at his current position and work on his idea on the side until he was earning enough money from it to pay his expenses every month. Once you are making enough money on your side gig to cover rent, food, debts, etc., it is time to make the jump.

Prepare to spend all of your free time, your nights, weekends, and holidays working on your idea or product. In addition, take a good look at your budget and get ready to strip it down as much as possible. The less your monthly expenses are, the quicker you can make that jump when your product or idea begins bringing in income. Remember once you make that jump, you most likely are not going to be earning anywhere near the amount you were making at your 9–5. Personally, I did not take a salary for the first year and a half after starting our lawn care business. Many times, business owners do not start earning good money until their second or third year of business, so you need to be aware of this ahead of time. Also, before you make the jump, while you are still working your 9–5, you may want to set up what I call a *blind* bank account. This account will be somewhat of a safety net and should have money automatically transferred to it on a regular basis that you basically forget exists. Most importantly, keep your eyes on your ultimate goal and work hard on your side hustle until you are earning enough money through it, and have some sort of safety net, before you make the jump. Because when you make that jump, an incredible new world is about to open up for you.

Action Steps and Reflection

Draw a Venn diagram and contemplate the three following areas—what are you good at, what can you be paid for, and what do you love to do. You may not have all three of these answers immediately; consider getting neutral outside opinions regarding what you are good at. Sometimes, an outsider can give us great insight as to our strengths.

Chapter 5

● ● ●

THE AMERICAN DREAM AND WORK

Imagine spending eight or more hours a day doing something you do not enjoy. For many people, this is a reality. They dislike their job and they feel like they have no way out. For me, the thought of spending the one life I get doing something I dislike or am not passionate about is a horrible thought—it is a wasted life. For many Millennials, they are wasting their youth, their energy, and some of the most valuable years of their life working at a 9–5 that produces income, which is the highest taxed form of profit. Doesn't the idea of spending a third of your life, eight hours a day, doing something that does not line up with your financial or life goals and values seem like a massive waste of time, resources, energy, and youth? This is the question every Millennial should be asking.

WORKING TO SPEND

Why does the average person living a middle class lifestyle have such a difficult time getting ahead, getting to the point where they have freedom in their life? For starters, most of them have terrible spending habits. Whether they are seeking out a loan for a car or a house, most people will want to know what is the maximum amount loan they can qualify for. Getting the nicer car and the bigger house is adding more stress to people's lives and maxing out their finances. We see disposable income at such a low percentage in the middle class. Because everyone is stuck in this mindset to spend excessively, most people can barely keep their heads above water. I see many people constantly striving for more, trying to chase this image of what they should have and living to impress their friends and family. Pursuing this American Dream of what you should have to show that you "made it" will never offer you the financial freedom you truly want.

To have this type of freedom, people need to begin running their personal finances like a business does. Most people I speak with do not know how much they spend, let alone keep a log of expenses or have any type of budgeting system. For business owners, knowing your numbers is important, whether it is how much your company spends on the phone bill each month or what employees' wages are each week. Knowing numbers is just as important for personal finances. What is your break-even point each month? How much money do you need to earn just to pay your monthly bills? You hear the term profit margins all the time in business, but when it comes to individual finances, how much money does someone need to make each month to hit zero, and then what is the percentage they are profiting monthly?

I tell many of my listeners who do not know their numbers and are in need of a budgeting system to find an app they like. It will be easily accessible on their phone, which most people have on them at all times. One of my favorites is an app called Mint. Apps like this allow people to categorize their expenses, see how much they are spending monthly, and then chart their saving and spending progress over time. They can also use these apps to set short- and long-term goals such as cutting down on expenses or increasing revenue for their personal finances.

Cutting back on expenses will not be an easy task at first. For most people living in the middle class lifestyle, they are spending up to 98 percent of their income! This does not leave much room for saving, whether for an entrepreneurial idea down the road, for retirement, or for an emergency. For someone who has a business or product idea and wants to take the "jump," income is going to be a tough road for a while and some may take a large pay cut or not be able to take a paycheck altogether. Learning how to lower expenses and save before taking the jump not only allows them to take more risks in business endeavors or investments, but it also allows someone to reach their goals quickly.

For younger people who want to start a business or, say, get involved in real estate, they must learn how to save money and live on as little as possible. When someone can successfully manage their expenses and learn how to live on little, they can then put everything they earn in excess of the amount they need to survive toward something worthwhile. For someone who can get concrete on their monthly numbers, when they have a numerical figure forecasted for a future goal, they can accurately project the time frame to reach that goal. They are setting the foundation for financial freedom and will have the ability to take larger risks. When Millennials can get by living on a little, they can chase what they love and possibly get paid big dividends down the road.

SLASHING THE BUDGET

For some people, one way to get out of the 9–5 and make the jump into entrepreneurship will be through building up a certain amount of money beforehand. One of the biggest hurdles in doing this is being married to the middle class lifestyle. I hear the same stories from many people who call into the podcast. Someone has debt, a mortgage, and a family to take care of and is spending over 90 percent of their income. While they may have a good paying job, they are accustomed to spending their money—most of it, in fact. They have allowed their lifestyle to adapt to their income level, and as their income increases, they keep making "improvements" in their lifestyle. Maybe it is a membership to a country club or gym, more vacations, or more clothes—whatever it may be, they just keep spending their money. My advice to Millennials is when your income increases, keep your lifestyle the same. Or better yet, find more areas in which to cut expenses and keep even more of your income. This is one of the best ways to save money and invest in your future.

One caller who was trapped in this type of situation sticks out in my mind. Kevin had a job, a small amount of student debt, and was living the typical middle class lifestyle, spending over 90 percent of his earnings. He had an amazing entrepreneurial idea for a product and had begun working on it in his free time. It was a body building-based product that was already beginning to do well, and after doing some calculations he projected he could earn around $40,000 the first year of its launch if he made the jump. The downside of this projection was his expenses were so high, he would literally be going into debt if he only earned $40,000 in the first year from this product. At the time Kevin called into the podcast, he felt like there was no way for him to chase after his dream. He was tied to his day job but was extremely passionate about exercise and the product he had created. He did not mind his job but he knew he wanted to create his own schedule and do something that was more aligned with his goals and interests. In addition, he wanted to spend more time with his family, as his current position had him working almost 60 hours a week and he was traveling nonstop. When he asked me what he should do, I told him he needed to get his expenses down to that $40,000 projection. This needed to be Kevin's target number, however, he was currently spending about $90,000 per year. I told him his options included the following: stay at your current job which you are not satisfied with, go into debt and fund your lifestyle with debt during the first few years of launching this product (not recommended), or genuinely try to scale back your lifestyle.

Kevin chose the last option and I worked with him on slashing his expenses. He had never looked closely at this budget and was not aware of how much he was spending each month on certain things. Even though he had created a budget of sorts in the past, this budget was set up for spending 90 percent of his income. We examined everything he spent money on over the past year such as entertainment, eating out, clothes, etc. We were able to list every category that involved spending and trimmed each category to some degree.

One of the larger budgeting items was his housing expenditure. He had built up equity in his home because he had bought it after the housing bubble. After realizing he could scale down a bit, he sold his four-bedroom house and moved his family into a three-bedroom home. His family has just leased two new cars, which is probably one of the worst financial decisions you can make. We decided he should get rid of them, even if he would be taking a loss. In return, he purchased some used vehicles that were several years old. At the end of our budgeting session, he was able to get his family's budget down to $40,000 per year. It was quite amazing. The greatest help in reaching this figure was being able to sell this man's home and make some profit. In the end, he was able to make the jump, start his company, and not go into debt. The first year, just as Kevin projected, was difficult. He made about $40,000 net profit. By the second year, he was already making more than he earned at his prior day job. Now his company has taken off and he is enjoying his life and his business.

In his case, if he had not been willing to cut back on expenses and make some major changes, he probably would have still enjoyed a decent lifestyle. His $100,000 a year position most likely would have offered him a few raises, but there would have been a cap down the road. With his new company, there was no ceiling as far as income. That is what is amazing about entrepreneurship—there is no ceiling as to what you can earn. The growth potential is there, and the harder you work and the more vision you have, the more money you might be able to generate. Even just from a financial standpoint, it is a much more rewarding life. As this caller increased his income each year, I encouraged him not to return to his previous lifestyle of spending. For a lot of people, they believe if they could just make more, they could finally save more. This is simply not the case; I have seen people who made $40,000 a year spend the same percentage of their money and display the same spending habits as they do when they were making $80,000 or $100,000 per year. There is a flaw in their mindset regarding spending that needs to be corrected. If people continue to have the same spending habits, they are going to spend the same percentage regardless of how much money they make. If they expect to live a particular lifestyle, have a certain vehicle, and a specific type of house, they are always going to live on the brink of financial disaster with little to no savings. Instead of focusing on the American Dream and what type of lifestyle they "should" have, Millennials need to begin determining how much money they need to get by each month and how they can save in order to pursue their dreams in the future. They should be constantly reminding themselves to keep their expenses low and now allow their income to dictate their lifestyle. Adopting this mindset and these habits will set you up for a much more financially secure future.

BUILDING YOUR RUNWAY

How much runway do you need to accomplish your dreams? In other words, how much savings do you need before you can make the jump from your 9–5 to some type of entrepreneurial pursuit? Think of your runway in terms of a 747. A 747 does not go straight up in the air, and most businesses will not do the same thing. But if you build up your runway, your safety net, you can save yourself from a crash landing. For the first year and a half after I started my company, I did not take a salary and instead put money back in to grow the business. You have to prepare for the fact that there will be an amount of time when first starting your project or company where earnings will not be high. People currently in a 9–5 situation must realize that pursuing their dream will not mean overnight success. You won't quit your job, start your business, and pull in an exorbitant amount of money instantly. It is vital that you do not run out of fuel during this time. My suggestion is people have enough "fuel" in their tanks to get them through the first two years of the business. In order to do this, you need to strip down your budget, strip down your spending, and maximize your savings and ultimately your runway length.

Action Steps and Reflection

What are some examples in your life where you saw people overspend, or saw people living a lifestyle based on their income instead of their net worth?

Do you consider yourself someone who overspends? Consider downloading a budgeting app such as Mint and track your expenditures for one week. Are there any areas in which you could strip down?

• • •

PART 2: BREAKING OUT OF THE MIDDLE CLASS

Chapter 6

● ● ●

GO BIG OR GO HOME

From a young age, so many of us are steered into pursuing small, achievable goals. One of the first defining questions we are asked is what we want to be when we "grow up." For some people that answer may be a doctor, and others it might be a teacher, police officer, or astronaut. We will be asked this question over and over again by our parents, teachers, and even our high school guidance counselors. And, no matter what our profession of choice is at that moment we answer, it is often met with the question of whether our goal is attainable and reasonable. I think in the back of people's minds, they are hoping the child being asked this question does not write down this massive goal and then be somehow disappointed because he or she cannot reach it. We have been falsely guided throughout most of our adolescence by those who believed they were giving us good advice: keep your dreams reasonable and average so they can be accomplished. This advice will get you nowhere...fast.

High school students are continuously sent mixed messages when it comes to goals. Young men and women are expected to wake up extremely early, come to school, work hard, and achieve good grades in their classes and on tests. However, at the same time they are being steered to have average goals, average levels of success in their careers, and fit in with everyone else. I do not know about you, but if I am expected to wake up at 6 a.m., it better be for something big and juicy and not something everything else is going after.

I encourage people to go after something big in life because that is what it takes to get someone out of bed in the morning, to get them to sacrifice their time and energy. When there is a big goal you are striving for, something almost seemingly unattainable by the standards of others, the desire to reach that goal is going to get you to do stuff you would not otherwise want to do. That is when you know your dream is big enough—when you are so driven to get there and make it happen, you are willing to sacrifice and put in the time.

Let's use an example of a young medical student who has this massive goal of becoming a doctor and curing Cancer. If this is someone's goal, it is going to motivate them to study, sacrifice, and lay aside friendships and their free time that could be spent doing a million other things because they know they have to study nonstop to pursue this goal. The goal is big and juicy enough and there is so much upside to it, so they are willing to put in the time and effort. Whereas, when people settle for average goals—say just getting through high school or making a solid $50,000 per year—they are not going to be as motivated to get out of bed early. They are not going to be motivated to sacrifice. I believe it is sacrifice or regret when it comes to achieving your goals…and you get to choose.

I speak with many Millennials in their 30s now and when they look back on their life, they voice a lot of regret. They have this regret because there was not a goal they were pushing after; there was nothing to sacrifice for and nothing to chase. At their age, many are now stuck in debt, trapped in a 9–5, or they forget what it was like when they were younger and had a passion they wanted to chase after. They forgot about the big dream—the big idea they had when they were teenagers—and they stopped running after it. The pursuit ended and they had not really gotten anywhere in life. And, they have come to the realization after all this time they had just gone in circles.

This was part of the motivation for writing this book. I hate to see people in their early to mid-30s that look back on their life and say, "I did not get anywhere." For some, they might have traveled a long distance, but they did not have any direction and kept going down the same roads. This happened because they did not have any big goals or motivators to give them a specific direction. They had nothing that forced them to push harder than everyone else. The reason that people like Steve Jobs and Bill Gates built these massive corporations is because they were the ones spending 100+ hours a week in a lab, working on code, etc. They had a big dream they were passionate about and did not listen to the noise of people telling them to go out and enjoy their life and stop being so obsessed about this one goal. If they had listened to those voices, we most likely would not have Apple and Microsoft today. We would not have all of these technologies and breakthrough solutions. All of these things came from an individual or group of individuals who focused on a massive goal, an idea, and ambition that was greater than themselves, and they did not stop until they reached it.

This is why I tell people to go big or go home. If you are not going to go big in life, you are going to go down an average road and essentially, you will be going home. You will "check out" if there is not enough upside to the goal you are working toward. And when you wake up at 30 years old, one of two things will happen—you will either realize you have not gone anywhere and accomplished anything or you will be a Gates or Jobs and will have created something special with your work and sacrifice. Whether you have created economic stimulus or financial freedom, or solved a worldwide problem or created a technological breakthrough, you will have done something extraordinary.

GOALS: DREAM BIG

Sometimes I get podcast callers who are young entrepreneurs discouraged because they feel they are too young, and therefore somehow handicapped from reaching their goal. I do not see youth as a handicap but as more of a USP. You are younger than the competition and it is a great way to differentiate yourself. When these men and women call in, they are often disappointed and wondering if their age or lack of experience is going to drag them down. I explain that if a young entrepreneur has a big dream and the energy to fuel it, and is not tied down with extra baggage financially such as a big mortgage or taking care of family members, he or she has a greater chance of attaining the goal because he or she has the freedom to chase after it. That is the benefit to youth—having the ability to chase your dreams without being tied down by baggage. When these types of callers come in, I love to encourage them to go after big goals with everything they have. They have so much less to lose and a lot more freedom than say someone who has car payments, dependents, and a mortgage.

I recognized my desire to pursue big goals when I was young. I touched on this briefly earlier, but when I had to interview for college at the age of 13, I received a lot of pushback on the goals I had set for myself. I loved medicine and wanted to do great things in the field of Multiple Sclerosis. My eyes were set for medical school and making advances for patients suffering from this disease. But where I had planned to take science and technology courses, I was being steered into taking art and literature courses. School personnel were not keen on me being so focused on one pathway. People forget that the person who dives deep into one discipline or subject is the person who can innovate and create change in that category. I still remember in that meeting for college as we were putting my schedule together, they were trying to encourage me to explore other disciplines. While their advice was not necessarily bad, I believe we have lost that wonderment and the way we used to look at the beauty of someone who is completely dedicated to one field, one goal, and one ambition. These people become the change-makers, the thought leaders, and the visionaries—why are we trying to mold them into everyone else? After this college meeting, I realized I was going to have big goals regardless of what I do in my life. That day I made a decision to not allow anyone to put a ceiling on my goals, on my standards, or what I want out of life. Regardless of your age and your ambitions, I want to encourage you to stop allowing others to dictate the size of your goals and dreams. Dream big and do not settle.

GOAL SETTING AND BEARING FRUIT

In 2014, a friend and I were traveling back from Malawi when I decided to flesh out some goals and financial projections for my landscaping company for the following five years. For the projections, I was writing down how many employees we would need, what our gross revenue would be, how many clients we would have, and how many locations we would need. Needless to say, I get pretty specific when it comes to my company projections.

As I created each category in an Excel spreadsheet on my iPad, my friend glanced over and said, "You're dreaming." My response was, "No. This will happen!" My goals for the company were not average and I was not willing to step down to what someone else's goals and standards were. If I was like most people, I probably would have been writing down numbers that seemed more attainable, maybe 150 percent of what we did the year before. Instead, I was writing down big goals in timeframes of up to five years. When my friend made his comment, he had specifically been looking at my monthly revenue projections at the five-year forward mark. It turned out, within just 16 months, my company had already achieved the four-year marker on that revenue goal. It just goes to show regardless of how big the objective is, if you continue to follow your passion and are willing to sacrifice and put forth the energy, you can achieve your goals—sometimes even sooner than you think.

OWN YOUR GOALS

If people took more responsibility and ownership of their goals, they would be so much more passionate about them and their goals would continue to grow. If someone, however, is working toward a goal set by their parents, friends, or school advisor, they might like to achieve it but they are certainly not going to sacrifice for it. When it comes to tasks like budget stripping and bringing down expenses in order to reach a goal, no one wants to do the work. People do not want to go through the pain of looking at every expense and every category down to the dollar. No one wants to sacrifice if there is no payoff or big goal to get to. I have given people this advice many times over but they do not follow it because their goal or dream they are envisioning is not big enough. It is not enough to get them excited or to sacrifice for in order to achieve it.

By giving others the chance to dictate your goals, or giving them the ability to lower the standards of your goals, you are putting your financial future in their hands. And by putting your security in their hands, you are allowing them to dictate whether you are going to be someone who pushes the limit and achieves their goals and financial freedom, or be the person who always had their goal in the back of their mind but never achieved anything because they were not willing to make sacrifices. I see a lot of young men and women allow someone else to set their goals for them. This happens often when it comes to education because they try to do what their parents have told them or what they believe would make their parents proud. They fall into this pattern of letting someone else dictate what their goals should be and in the end are taking their security, happiness, and financial future out of their own hands.

Like I always tell my podcast listeners, no one is as motivated to reach someone else's goals as they are to reach their own. Make sure your ideas and goals are big enough to motivate you and fire you up and do not back down when someone tries to persuade you to go in a different direction.

Action Steps and Reflection

Think about a time in life, perhaps in school or in your career, when you set a goal and achieved or succeeded that goal in record time. Use similar strategies and create a plan for reaching one of your larger life goals or dreams you wrote down previously.

Chapter 7

● ● ●

THE BIG THREE

Many Millennials come to me regarding the same career advice: How can they determine the career that would work best for their needs and personality, while also giving them the financial freedom they desire? I share the same exercise with each of them. Closely examine the following three questions: What are you good at? What are you passionate about? What can you be paid for? The easiest way to see where these three categories line up is to create a Venn diagram and input your answers.

A lot of times, people go to school and only consider what can pay the bills when it comes time to determine their career choice. If people really considered these three areas, they could focus on where they want to go and how they are going to get there. Success, or that sweet spot where all three categories intersect, is not going to come right away, but as long as you have a clear path of where you want to be headed and what it is going to involve, you can start moving in the right direction.

Depending on how old you are when you complete this type of Venn diagram will have a large impact on your answers, so you may find yourself fine tuning these three categories over time. As you mature and grow and gain more life experience, you will have a better idea regarding your talents, what you truly enjoy doing, and what you can be paid to do. Age is not a requirement to fill in this diagram; your answers mature as you develop. At the beginning, if the person contemplating these three areas is someone younger without much business experience, their graph is going to look a certain way. It may change and evolve, which is fine, as long as those changes focus on this individual's ultimate goal and what he or she is passionate about, and aren't about collecting a paycheck and just making the bills.

If you are younger and are still contemplating what you are good at in life, now may be a great opportunity to ask some friends and family members. What do you think they would say? The answers may surprise you. Whether you have great fashion sense or are good at fixing cars and electronics, asking those closest to you for their unbiased opinion may be helpful when it comes time to examining the "big three" categories.

GETTING TO WHERE YOU'RE GOING

When you first graduate high school or college, you cannot expect to be paid for something you love and are passionate about right away. In rare occasions this may happen but it is not the norm. I am passionate about biotech and also helping people in third world countries. When I was 16 or 17, I could not do things right away in those areas (such as build an orphanage). I had to determine what I could get paid for because I was good at it and at the time the answer was lawn care. This is why I initially went into lawn care, because I knew it was something I could be paid for and it was something that came easy to me. I was good at it and had been doing it well since I was a preteen. Then, as time progressed, I began doing things I was more passionate about, such as the podcast and creating BioShakes. The progression in terms of hitting that sweet spot where all three categories intersect is gradual.

It is wrong to feel like you are entitled to achieve that intersection immediately when you are first starting out. It is cocky to assume you are going to finish school and land the best job doing something you have always loved or be a top ranking musician or artist right off the bat. There needs to be some work, sweat, and sacrifice involved. It was not my dream to make lawn stripes straighter, but it was a stepping-stone to get me to where I wanted to be. Success will not happen overnight and you are going to have to put in the hours and gain the experience. If you want to start a business, you are going to have to raise the capital, which is what I am doing now. I am generating funds from something I am not super passionate about (lawn care), but it fills the categories of what I am good at and what I can be paid for. And through these funds I have been able to create something that aligns more with my passions—my BioShakes business and the podcast.

It is important to realize from the get-go you might be working as grunt labor, you might be in an internship you do not truly love, or you might be working a job that does not bring in much income. What you are learning in all of these different experiences are valuable skills, perhaps being mentored, or gaining industry knowledge that is going to help you later when it comes time to jump into something you are good at, passionate about, and can be paid to do. So keep your big goals in the forefront of your mind and do not give up —just remember they will not come to fruition overnight. We all have to start somewhere, and it is usually at the bottom. Put in the work and you can see a rewarding payoff in the end.

PREPARE FOR THE JOURNEY

Building a successful business or getting to a high level in your career will take hard work. Some Millennials are living an illusion that it will somehow be handed to them. Some of this is tied back to our educational system, where students have counselors and teachers holding their hands the entire way and pushing them along. When the time comes to enter the real world, these men and women get a reality check that they will have to fend for themselves. Everything will not be given to them. Everything is not explained somewhere in a syllabus. You do not have counselors guiding you along the way. Information will not be regurgitated from a professor and then given to you so you can pass your test. There will come a point when you begin your career and are ready to run toward your goal that you have to take ownership of your career and life.

So much is given to us for free in today's society that many of us get stuck in this cycle believing we are entitled to free stuff. There is a belief that we should not have to sacrifice for much. That is a dangerous position to be in as an entrepreneur when you are trying to build a business and aiming to reach goals. You must realize that what you love and have always dreamed of doing will in no way be handed to you on a silver platter and people are not going to walk with you hand in hand along in your journey. There will be a lot of struggle, pain, and sacrifice and you may be alone a large portion of the way. A payoff will most likely be seen if you continue pursuing, but you need to accept early on that a long, potentially difficult road is ahead of you.

DELAYED VS. INSTANT GRATIFICATION

You say you want to be a successful entrepreneur. In addition to making more sacrifices than the average person, you must also embody different character traits and habits. If you study the behavior of most CEOs, you will find they are early risers, they stick to routines, they exercise and take care of their body, they meditate, and they read. In fact, reading is a main area I would like to examine more. Did you know according to Refreshleadership.com, CEOs read an average of

60 books per year? Quite a different number compared to your average person who reads between one and six books per year. CEOs are always gaining knowledge and constantly learning. Many of these CEO behaviors are not shared by those who are less successful. Why? Simple—they are not willing to sacrifice. They do not want to wake up early, go to the gym, form a routine, and consistently better themselves through learning. Millennials can propel themselves to the positions they admire by adopting some of these same behaviors and sacrificing certain things in life in order to improve.

Millennials also need to learn the concept of delayed gratification. I see a lot of resumes of Millennials who are jumping around to many different jobs. Quite often, they expected their job to be something different than what it was. They will quit a great job that offered incredible learning opportunities because they expected it to be better. Yes, Millennials should have goals and an idea of what their career should look like, but there has to be delayed gratification and a season where you put your head down and grind it out. There are going to be times when you have to work harder than someone else at something you do not enjoy. This is all part of the journey. Delayed gratification is part of being able to sacrifice now for a larger benefit down the road.

Instant gratification is another concept that we need to discuss. Let's say someone graduates from college and is debt-free. She can finish school and get a job or start building her own business. Instant gratification would be taking the job because that person immediately sees a paycheck, vacation time, healthcare, and benefits. An entrepreneur will consider starting a business and prepare themselves for potentially not earning a salary right away, putting in twice as many hours, having no vacation and living off little money. When you look at these two options, most people will choose the job because it is easier. You start getting paid shortly after you begin working. It is these scenarios in which you have to ask yourself, "Am I willing to delay gratification and sacrifice now for a better future?"

You have seen my favorite maxim mentioned several times throughout the book—sacrifice or regret, you choose. When you delay gratification, you might have to sacrifice a lot now but later down the road you will look back and you will not regret the choices you made. When people choose the road of instant gratification, they often look back on their choice and have many regrets. I see it over and over with the people I meet and those who call into the podcast. Choosing what looked like an easier road led to a lot of anguish in the end.

A lot of Millennials have to make this choice when it comes to their careers. They have to make a choice of whether they are going to jump right into the middle class dream and possible regret it later on, or work hard for a better payout in the end. The reason the entire middle class mindset is so attractive is because it seems that you can accomplish it relatively easily. If you get a decent education and graduate, you could potentially begin making $70,000+ a year and essentially you have instantly become "middle class." To get to this same position as an entrepreneur may take more time—a few years in fact—but at some point you will surpass the other person and have many more freedoms that are not available to them. Entrepreneurs understand they will not see the benefits right away, and there is more work involved on their journey, but it reaps more reward down the road.

WHAT IS A MILLENNIAL MILLIONAIRE?

The definition of the term "Millennial Millionaire" is someone is who still considered young but has reached a high level of success. This "success" does not necessarily have to be money. There are many different ways to measure success, but this term encapsulates someone who has reached success at an early age and who does not have many regrets because they shot for the stars and went for something big. Millennial Millionaires chase after something they are passionate about; they are willing to set aside current gains for the future and push away the idea of instant gratification. By doing these things, they have gained success in their field and reached a level beyond their peers. This term also embodies anyone who has reached the point where their three circles, their three categories, intersect. Their success is not so much a dollar amount as it is a place—a place where they do what they love, they are passionate about their endeavors, and they are getting paid. In that sphere, in that zone, that person can reach their full potential. They can help mankind. They can become an innovator. They can create solutions to the problems in our environment or our healthcare system. They have harnessed all three categories to create something extraordinary.

Action Steps and Reflection

Create your own personal definition of a Millennial Millionaire using the goals and dreams you aspire to achieve. Keep this definition handy and read it often for inspiration.

• • •

PART 3: HABITS OF THE MILLENNIAL MILLIONAIRE

Chapter 8

● ● ●

DO MILLENNIALS RENT OR BUY?

With homeownership being so heavily woven into the image of the American Dream, many Millennials come to me regarding advice on buying a house. Often times, I will meet or hear from young entrepreneurs who are great at running a business and terrific at making money, but they make extremely poor decisions when it comes to housing. Many call into the podcast and discuss this massive anchor that is ruining their financial picture—their mortgage. In order to be successful, I discuss how people need three major areas of their life—their home, education, and career—to be serving them rather than the other way around. I have seen countless people become slaves to their mortgages, their jobs, and degrees that are doing nothing for them. It is time to flip our mindset and make these things work for us rather than against us.

This is why the purchasing vs. renting conversation is so important, especially for young people who are just graduating from college, starting their first job, or beginning their own business. The housing process can either be a rewarding step in their financial journey or it can be an anchor and a detriment. If done incorrectly, it could put someone into bankruptcy and set them back financially eight years

or more. Housing is a huge investment and is one of the most important decisions each one of us will make at some point in our life.
Purchasing a home will also be most people's largest ticket item and,
because homeownership is inherently tethered to this broken image
of the American Dream, many people forget how much of their net
worth will be tied up in this purchase.

For a long time before the housing market crashed, people were
overconfident that housing prices would continue to soar. The reality
is, no matter where you are investing your time, money, or energy,
you need to prepare yourself beforehand for the worst-case scenario.
Whether you are discussing housing, career, or an education, sit
down and consider the upsides and downsides to each. For instance,
with education, your worst-case scenario is wasting four to six years
earning a degree and then possibly not finding a job or not enjoying
what you are doing with the degree afterward. With your career, the
worst-case scenario is being stuck in a 9–5 you dislike and/or are not
being paid well. And for housing, the worst-case is over-leveraging
yourself, not being able to pay off your mortgage, not being able to
rent the home to cover the mortgage, and potentially having to file
bankruptcy. You also have to consider the possibility of getting a better opportunity in another location and determining if you are able
to make that jump if you are locked into a home in a specific locale.
Honestly analyzing the worst-case scenarios helps you determine your
risk and figure out if and how you are able to protect your downside.
Not knowing this ahead of time can cause a lot of heartache down the
road.

In the world of startups and entrepreneurship, you see a lot of
the "try, fail, repeat" mindset—you failed but at least you obtained
experience throughout the process. When it comes to housing, this is
a terrible model to follow. Failing at home investments can cost you,
big time. You cannot just wash your hands of a $400,000 mortgage

and say, "Whoops. Made a mistake on that one," and move on. You will pay in some way, whether by ruining your finances to bringing stress into your family and relationships. For Millennials and first time home buyers, the major decision of purchasing a home can make or break the first 10 or 20 years of their financial freedom and is not a decision that should be taken lightly. And while learning from your past mistakes and failures is a popular theme we hear often from business leaders, when it comes to housing, I would rather learn from other people's failures. If we look back to 2008, we can all learn a lot from the people whose lives and businesses were ruined from the catastrophic housing crash. We do not have to be the one to pave the road of experience because it has already been done and we should be mindful of the lessons they learned.

DOWNSIDE OF A MORTGAGE

If someone is dead set on purchasing a house, I ask them if they had to rent out the home, could they cover the mortgage? If we use 2008 as an indicator, we see countless people who bought $300,000 and $400,000 homes which, after the crash, were renting for $1,500 when their mortgages were double and triple this amount. People took these massive zero percent down mortgages from banks hook, line, and sinker. In the end, they paid an extremely high price—their financial freedom. So, taking the lessons learned from 2008, for anyone interested in purchasing single family residences, you need to make sure you can cover your downsides.

For those who are interested in truly investing their money, I recommend looking at multi-family housing units in which I apply the 50 percent rule. I would never purchase an investment property that only covered the mortgage if I had to rent it out. To me, that is a major red flag. If I find a duplex that catches my eye, I would need to rent both units out for enough money that half of that amount would cover the mortgage and the remaining half would go toward expenses, property taxes, and profit. When someone tells me about this great homeownership deal they found and we discuss whether they can cover their mortgage through renting, if I learn they cannot, I would consider that endeavor to be very risky and unwise.

In addition to covering their downsides regarding home ownership, Millennials also need to keep in mind that many businesses are going global thanks to the Internet and technology. Because of this, people need to be mobile. Today, Millennials will have more jobs out of any generation. Where people used to have one or two jobs throughout their life, most Millennials will have more than ten various positions. With this as today's reality, we must keep in mind that a massive mortgage may keep us from expanding and reaching new experiences, getting a promotion, or doing something we are more passionate about. Of course on the other hand, you can be in the midst of a great housing market and sell your house for a profit, but since we cannot put all of our confidence in an ever-growing housing market, we must analyze the situation and be able to cover our downsides. Being over-leveraged and tied down is one of the most common scenarios I hear about when people call into the podcast. They cannot chase an experience or a dream because of a mortgage that ties them down to a physical location. This is another unforeseen cost of owning a mortgage that many do not consider.

BUYING VS. RENTING

One the most popular questions I receive is whether someone should purchase a home or rent one. Let's take a closer look at the outflow of money for each decision. For this, we will assume someone has a good credit score of 740 and is going to put down 20 percent, $60,000, on a $300,000 home. If they choose to rent, we will assume their initial outlay will be last month's rent and security deposit at a total of $2,000. We will also take a look at what would happen if they took their initial outlay to purchase the home—$60,000—and placed that money into a mutual fund or portfolio that is making 8 percent.

Let's see what happens with this $60,000 if it is used to purchase a home. This person is assuming a 30-year mortgage with a 5 percent interest rate. Their monthly payment is $1,288. Their principal is now $240,000, less the $60,000 down payment, but over 30 years, their interest payments will amass to $223,000. Property taxes would be approximately $130,000. Then you need to add in repairs, insurance, a new roof, appliances, and maintenance over 30 years. When you add all of these things together, you have spent approximately $793,814 over the course of three decades for a home that was originally $300,000.

For this example, we will assume the house doubles in value in 30 years time, so it is now worth $600,000. Most people will see this figure and think it is wonderful that their property doubled in value; however, they are actually in the negative $193,000 because of all of the other costs that have compiled throughout the years. It is for this reason that I feel investing in SFRs can actually be a liability in the end. With renting, you see the amount you spent renting for 30 years, $120,000 give or take, but you are taking away the bulk of responsibilities that come with owning a home and all of the extra costs associated with it, not to mention you have more flexibility regarding moving. When it comes to investing the initial outlay of $60,000, most people would be better off locking it up for 30 years in a mutual fund or investment portfolio and letting it grow into what could potentially be over $600,000, assuming an 8 percent return.

While this chart is full of assumptions, and in some places rent is higher than what is stated here, it is more of an example to challenge the idea that homeownership is so much more financially prudent than renting 100 percent of the time. Like most things in life, of course there are exceptions. Sometimes you can find a certain property or fixer-upper for a good deal, and with a little sprucing up, can be quickly sold for a profit. However, if you are bent on purchasing a home you have to take into account the possibility of the real estate market not going up continually, and all of the additional expenses and costs that come with homeownership.

When I am speaking to a Millennial who is considering the purchase of a SFR, I make sure he or she sees the property as a potential liability because of the upkeep, maintenance, taxes, and other costs that will be incurred. There are just so many expenses revolving around this type of housing. Now if you consider a duplex, triplex, and so on, you can essentially make it a cash flow positive investment. My suggestion is people who are trying to build their career and be cash flow positive should consider purchasing an investment property as their first housing purchase. They can purchase a duplex using a 3.5 percent down FHA loan, live in one unit, and rent out the other. That other rented unit is essentially paying off the mortgage every month, allowing you to live cash flow neutral while the mortgage is being met.

Over time, if you plan to start a family, you may not want to live next door to someone, so I suggest you make a commitment to live there for two years out of five and then sell the property without paying capital gains. If you need or want to sell it before the two-year commitment mark, you can sell it as a 1031, which allows investors to take any money they receive from an investment deal and essentially roll it into another investment deal, tax free. You need to set up a 1031 with a bank before you sell your property. To learn more about this, I suggest visiting Biggerpockets.com and listening to their advice on this topic.

The money you receive can then be used to purchase something bigger, say with five or more units, through a commercial loan the second time around. Beginning the home purchasing process with a duplex is a great way for Millennials to get started in real estate. It provides someone with valuable landlord and management experience and it is a way to stay invested in the market. Getting a loan for a duplex will even prove easier for someone getting their feet wet in the real estate market. Say someone had just graduated college, is earning $50,000 per year, and is interested in purchasing a duplex, renting out one side for $1,500 per month. The bank will take this expected profit and multiply it by 12, giving you $18,000, and will add that amount to your income when you apply for the loan. How they envision it is you are going to be making money on this real estate purchase, so your annual income is going to increase, which will further allow you to qualify for the loan. Multifamily dwellings are also recession proof. When the housing market tanks, people have to downsize or are forced to rent because they cannot get a loan, which makes your property a hot commodity. When the housing market is going well, rents continue to increase—a win-win for you in either situation. The bottom line is that multifamily dwellings are a good investment idea for any Millennial wanting to become involved in the real estate market and should be considered first before moving onto a single family residence.

Action Steps and Reflection

Do your own research regarding the expenses involved in home ownership by speaking with a friend or family member who has owned property for a substantial amount of time.

Inquire about the expenses involved in purchasing and keeping a home in good condition. Compare these expenses and any profit made to someone who owns a duplex or triplex. What advantages and disadvantages do you see between the two?

Chapter 9

● ● ●

DO MILLENNIAL MILLIONAIRES GO TO COLLEGE?

I s there an entrepreneurial way to think about college? Simply put, yes. Let's begin by running the numbers. HSBC published a report in 2014 detailing the average cost of college in various locations throughout the world. The United States landed in the number three spot for most expensive options (this combined college tuition and living expenses), with an estimated annual cost of $36,564. This was a median figure, with some private institutions costing more and public colleges averaging less. If we break this annual figure down to $3,000 out-of-pocket each month and consider placing this money into a mutual fund or real estate investment making 8 percent, rather than spending it on tuition and living expenses, we would have a profit of somewhere around $170,167 after four years rather than the same amount in student loan debt (not to mention the amount of money that could have been earned during these school years).

The question for Millennials is do they need to go to college to reach their goals or would it be prudent for them to begin working, gaining experiences and skills, and saving their money rather than going into debt?

Because most students finance their college education, and college is typically five to six years rather than a squeaky clean four years, careful consideration must be made regarding someone putting their financial future at risk and amassing tens or hundreds of thousands of dollars in student loans. And with almost 50 percent of college graduates unable to secure a job in the field they studied or being grossly underpaid, is spending the next ten or more years paying off student loans the financially prudent thing to do?

Just as we had spoken about some of the negative side effects that come with locking yourself into a home purchase, such as not being able to move or chase after a different opportunity in another location, college also comes with drawbacks. During these prime college years you could be gaining real-world experiences and application, which is crucial for a young entrepreneur. At a time when one has the most energy and not much holding them down, they could be gaining skills, meeting key people, and gaining a foothold in a specific industry. The four to six years that may be spent earning a college degree could also be spent getting established in your industry, learning from people who are influential, and perhaps starting your own business or brand. It is an injustice to the young people in our society when we push them into an educational system that is getting more and more expensive and is becoming more and more questionable regarding whether or not it is actually teaching them what they need to know to secure a job.

I believe from the ages of 18 to 25 someone is in the prime years of their life regarding learning and building relationships. This time period can set people up for the rest of their lives. These years can be the most impactful and resourceful in terms of gaining experiences in business and getting ahead in your own passion projects. You really have to ask if spending all of your energy and passion reading a textbook or regurgitating information for a test is a gross waste of your talent, vigor, and time.

EDUCATION VS. EXPERIENCE

According to a 2013 study by the National Center for Education Statistics, 33.5 percent of Americans ages 25 to 29 had earned at least a Bachelor's degree by 2012. Compare this to 1975's share, which was 21.9 percent having earned at least a Bachelor's degree, and you can see how just a generation ago someone's educational level was a large part of their USP. Having earned a four-year degree several decades ago would have impressed most employers, but today employers are examining someone's experiences more closely. Questions asked during interviews are changing and employers want to see how someone would react in management situations and real-world scenarios—two skill areas that cannot be learned through a textbook.

If the idea of pursuing entrepreneurship draws you in, then you need to place yourself in a situation where you will begin to learn about starting a business, managing different types of people, overseeing financials, managing a website, and more, and most of this you will not learn in a classroom. Spending your prime "college" years working as an entrepreneur and training in the real world essentially offers you a mini-accounting or management degree by the time four years have passed. The hands-on, practical experience you will gain will not only impress future employers (if working for a corporation is your goal), but can also propel you closer to your dreams of business ownership and being an entrepreneur. In today's corporate world, we are seeing more interest in what skills, experiences, and resources someone has over what grades they received and degree they earned. It is time to consider and question which road—college or real world experience—has more value.

As an employer, if I was hiring and had to compare someone who had six years of entrepreneurial experience, team building, selling, and growing a company over someone who had six years of college experience and a degree in Communications or Humanities, I would see more value in the candidate with real-world experience. To me, that individual's knowledge would be more significant in terms of their potential to grow and improve my company.

Even if your goal is not owning your own company but rather working for a corporation, learning these skills and having hands-on training in areas such as sales, management, financial understanding, and so on is what will bring value to a company. Much of what we learn in textbooks and a classroom doesn't necessarily move the needle, which is why we find a certain type of employee getting cut first during a recession. They are not "moving the needle" in terms of bringing in more sales, driving revenue and business growth, and are not bringing unique ideas to the table. The people who are accomplishing these things are the entrepreneurs—those who can grind it out, figure out new paths to opportunities, determine cost/benefit analysis of new business ideas, and be innovative. Those are the skills one must possess in order to keep a company moving forward in today's economy.

In a recession, the employees who are terminated first are the people who just get by, do the bare minimum to get through the 9–5, and do not go above and beyond. The one with the entrepreneurial mindset, however, will push the envelope, grow the business, and solve the problem, which is why this mentality (combined with real-world training) is becoming more valuable than a degree.

Is a degree crucial in certain circumstances? Absolutely. If you are someone with a desire to become a physician, lawyer, or an engineer, for example, you need a degree. I am not against someone going to college if it aligns with their passion and ultimate goal; what I am against is when college is treated as this funneling system that people follow because "everyone else is doing it." People need to start evaluating the cost-benefit analysis of a college education (and the loans that come with it) and determine if it aligns with their life goals. If it does not, I highly recommend someone not following this typical college education route because ultimately they are putting their financial future in jeopardy.

FOLLOW A LEADER

If someone has to struggle with years of student loan debt repayment to attend college, isn't it time to begin questioning the value of that endeavor? For those who have been offered scholarships and financial aid, and do not have the desire to be an entrepreneur, college might be the right fit. But for those with big ideas and a goal to build their own business, to put all of that on hold and at the same time potentially go into debt, that decision is simply unwise. If someone has an entrepreneurial mindset but does not have funding after they graduate high school, my advice to him or her is to find a position at a startup. Move to Silicon Valley or a similar locale and gain exposure, experience, and skills. There is no better way to begin your own startup in the future than by learning all of the components necessary through hands-on training. This is more valuable than spending large amounts of money and going into debt to earn a piece of paper.

Now, are there people who should consider college after high school? Absolutely. This includes those who currently do not have direction. For this segment of the population, college can be a terrific vehicle to help them determine what they are passionate about. By examining different topics and industries, college may help these men and women fill in those three circles I discussed earlier—what are they passionate about, what are they good at, and what can they be paid to do. But for those with a dream and passion, I say chase after it or pursue an opportunity such as working with a startup or under a business leader where you can gain massive experience and skills and build your career on them.

A PATH LESS TRAVELED

While my college experience and timeline is different than most people I meet, determining the value of education over experience is crucial no matter your age or life path. Once I had decided I would not pursue medical school, I really began to question the money I was paying each month for tuition and whether or not it would be smarter to put that money into a real estate deal or new business venture.

People just graduating from high school need to think about whether or not having their heads in a book for the next four years is the right decision. College is a possibility, as is working for a startup or entrepreneurial business owner. Some men and women coming out of high school do not have a goal and are unsure about their passions. But for most of you reading this book, you do have a passion or a business idea. If I am describing you, my advice is to go out and gain experience. Pour your energy, time, passion, and thoughts into what keeps you up at night, what keeps your head spinning with ideas. Now is the time to question whether you want to spend the next four to six years of your life in an educational system that might not help prepare you for a career and may put you into debt for the next ten years. When you are at the crossroads of applying to college, ask yourself this: Do I want to spend the prime years of my life—my energy and building my career—working toward a degree or working toward my dream?

Action Steps and Reflection

Ask yourself if you need to go to college in order to reach your goals. If the answer is no, evaluate and research your next steps. Should you intern or work at a startup or for a company that sparks your interest? Is now the right time to step out and begin building your own business?

Chapter 10

● ● ●

DO MILLENNIAL MILLIONAIRES SAVE OR SPEND?

Truth be told, we live in a society of spenders. So when someone wants to fund a new business venture or finally be debt free, they often call my podcast and ask how they can make this goal a reality. I have been blessed to work with countless individuals and couples who trusted me with their financial situation and debt and many of the results have been incredible. When someone finally reaches out to me, they are often at their lowest point financially and extremely frustrated. Many of them have an incredible idea or business they want to pursue but they see no way of getting out the of 9–5 lifestyle. In order to help them bring their idea to fruition, I work with them on the process of stripping down their finances. It can be a tumultuous endeavor, but for those who are truly passionate about breaking free of any debt, chasing after a dream, or saying goodbye to their 9–5 routine, it is possible.

Over the years of working with people one-on-one, I have learned that the more passionate someone is about pursuing their passion, the more likely they are to strip down to financial basics. Desperation for change directly correlates with how much they are willing to strip out of their budget. If someone is truly sick and tired of living in debt and discontentment, they are willing to make sacrifices. For someone with a goal of saving an extra $5,000 per year or paying off the last of their student loans, it does not take much sacrifice or budget cutting. However, if someone wants to break free of a large amount of debt, save money for an entrepreneurial endeavor, or step away from their current employment, and is fed up with their lifestyle, these are the people who need to be willing to do whatever it takes in terms of sacrifice to get where they want to be. Often times, these men and women just need to be encouraged by a neutral outsider who reminds them that achieving these goals is possible. It may take extreme sacrifice, such as selling a home, a car, not eating out, skipping entertainment options, and canceling subscriptions to things like Netflix and Hulu. And while some people will drag their feet because they feel deprived of life's "simple pleasures" that make them happy, at some point they typically come to the realization that debt is not making them happy. In fact, it is usually ruining their life.

How much you are willing to sacrifice typically boils down to the state of your career, finances, and life. Hate all of those areas enough and you will be willing to lay aside all of the things that are weighing on your budget. Stripping down typically involves three areas of someone's life—their housing, their transportation, and their level of leisure activities. For many people, the housing aspect involves downsizing and selling items in the home that have accumulated over the years. Downsizing to a smaller home and lot means less money is spent in monthly mortgage costs, maintenance, and servicing the house and yard. And moving to a somewhat less upscale area, as humbling as that can be, often times brings with it less pressure of having to own the nicest vehicle on the block, the most extravagant landscaping, etc. For someone stuck in a large house with a massive mortgage, I would suggest one of two things: sell the home and move into a smaller, single family home in a simpler neighborhood or, and this is the better option in my opinion, purchase a duplex for virtually the same amount. As discussed in a previous chapter, the duplex offers you a roof over your head while someone else pays your mortgage by renting out the second unit. Sometimes, you can even earn a profit at the end of the month. Bottom line, when you strip down in the housing department, you can save a good amount of money.

Vehicles are right behind housing when I am working with someone in stripping down their budget. For some people, this is the area where they get tripped up the most. Why? Because a vehicle is often tied to a person's social and financial status. It is an appearance issue and a nice vehicle can make some people feel more accepted and accomplished. Now, when it comes to leasing a car versus purchasing one, leasing is a terrible decision, especially for people who want to get out of debt. Regardless if they have a lease or a purchased vehicle, they need to sell it or return it to the dealer. Yes, you'll lose money initially, but if you leased a vehicle, you are already losing money and if you purchased a new car and have a car payment, that vehicle has depreciated and lost money. In return, you can purchase a car that is worth somewhere between $7,000 and $12,000 and is more than four years old (the fastest rate of depreciation occurs in the first four years). Making major changes in this area can also lead to a sizable amount of savings over time.

Last, it is time to examine habits for entertainment, leisure activities, eating out, purchasing clothes, and all of the little expenses like coffee on the go and grabbing unnecessary items while in the checkout line. With fashion for example, I can usually work with clients to cut out up to 80 percent of their clothing budget. When it comes to small impulse purchases like coffee or bottles of water, people fail to realize those expenses add up at the end of the month. Through working on slashing expenses in each of these three areas for an average of six months, it is not rare for me to see someone be able to cut their budget by 50 percent!

When I explain the process to people and the sacrifice often involved, I typically get one of two responses. They either feel like they are being sent to a prison of sorts or they think the entire endeavor is impossible. The truth is, when you get to the point where you hate your job, are tired of being in financial despair, and are over the 9–5 grind, you will be driven to sacrifice. As I mentioned earlier, sacrifice or regret, you choose. Are you going to make the necessary changes today or are you going to do it in ten years? If you wait another ten years will you look back with regret and wished you would have done it sooner? I tell every person who comes to me with the desire to strip down their budget that we will work together to cut their expenses and, in a year or two, they are going to be extremely happy with the results.

ENJOYING THE REWARD

A while back, Daniel called into the podcast inquiring about stripping down expenses in order to chase after this product he invented, which are plyometric boxes that could be used at the home or gym. At the time, he was making $120,000 annually and we ended up stripping down his budget so he could live off $40,000. We estimated this would be his profit during his first year in business. In addition to cutting expenses, I also pushed him to design his product in a way that made it shippable. Eventually, Daniel created a product that could be folded but was sturdy when assembled. Now he was able to mass market the product and ship to any location rather than being trapped in a local market. By stripping down his budget and having an even better product ready to go, he was able to make the jump several years earlier than he had originally planned.

During the first year of this endeavor, he earned around $50,000, which is what we had calculated. By the second year, he was already making around $140,000. By stripping down and learning how to survive on a smaller budget, someone can jump into their entrepreneurial dream with the understanding that they won't make a large salary, if any, that first year. By working with this individual and preparing him to live on $40,000 annually, he was able to survive his first year as a business owner and is now reaping the reward.

THE PATH TO INVESTING

In addition to questions about cutting expenses, a popular topic I hear often on the podcast is whether someone should save or invest. When it comes to budgeting, we are always focused on saving money and determining ways to increase our savings. However, while I stress savings to everyone I counsel, I also want them to be aware that saving money in a checking or savings account is the most expensive form of creating wealth because it is taxed so heavily. Billionaires typically do not have pots of money sitting around—what they do have are investments, and lots of them. You need to be saving money in order to invest it. Personally, I may strip down my budget so my savings can be invested into one of three things: another company, something that will grow my current business, or a real estate deal. By taking this savings and putting it into my business, I can grow the business and also write it off as an expense. Real estate opportunities offer another way of shielding money from income taxes, etc. I do not ever save money with the sole intention of letting it sit and I always have an investing plan for any money I do save. What people do with their savings plays a large part on their overall financial picture. Keep in mind the wealthiest one percent of people put an average of 75 percent of their savings into investment assets. They do not keep it as liquid cash in their bank accounts but rather put it right back into stocks, real estate, and businesses. Now for those in the middle class mindset, the average amount of money typically left over for savings after expenditures is only two percent. This figure gives us an honest look at how many people in our society are obsessed with pointless consumption, and at the end of the day they are left with a lot of "things" but little to no savings for investment assets.

I mentioned this earlier, but one great way to get started with saving money is by setting up a blind account, which involves making weekly or monthly deposits and basically pretending the money does not exist. You do not track this money or add it to your budgeting and banking apps or trackers. The goal is to not have this money constantly visible, as that makes you more prone to spend it.

The money essentially goes into your blind account, and although you have access to it, you let it accumulate until you have reached your goal. This "goal" is whatever amount you need to fund a new business endeavor, grow your existing business in some way, or make a purchase in the real estate market.

There are three major investing endeavors that each offers a certain amount of risk but also an opportunity to gain experience and potentially make a profit. Investing in a new business can be especially risky, as the majority of small companies (80 percent according to Bloomberg.com) fail in their first 18 months, but it will give a young entrepreneur the greatest amount of experience. Real estate may be boom or bust, but statistically it is a safer investment than starting a business. Stocks or paper assets are easy investments because the time requirement is minimal compared to how much work is involved in starting your own business or managing real estate deals. With stocks and paper assets, however, you on average will not see the same large returns as you would when owning your own business or certain real estate ventures, but you will notice there is less risk involved.

Finally, when you have begun the investment process, I suggest exhausting your business first and putting as much money, energy, time, and passion into it as possible before moving on to the real estate market. Then, when your time is maxed out between business and real estate dealings, you will be well on your way to becoming a mature investor and will want to make your money work for you. That is the time to begin investing in stocks and bonds and other startups so your money is working hard while you are busy achieving success on your passion projects.

Action Steps and Reflection

How desperate are you to make a life change? Consider how stripping down your budget may help you achieve your goals. Be sure to add a budgeting app in order to keep track of your expenses, and consider setting up a blind account to save money and get you closer to reaching your goal.

Conclusion

● ● ●

WHAT DO YOU WANT OUT OF LIFE?

If you are reading this book, there is a great probability that you are already entrepreneurial driven and willing to sacrifice to achieve your dreams and passions. Plus, if you made it all the way to this conclusion, then I would bet you are the type of person who follows through and succeeds often in life. That being said, you might be asking what is the next step? For starters, it is time to give some serious thought to your concrete goals and begin organizing your life around them. Most people do not spend a good amount of time, if any, thinking about their concrete goals. I believe the journey begins when you know what you want out of life and can easily fill in those three circles we discussed previously. Those answers will help you determine what type of business you should start, how much income you need to produce, and what you ultimately want out of life.

You should also know your numbers at this point. By this, I mean you should have a concrete plan regarding how much money you need every month to reach your goals, attain the lifestyle you want, support your family, help the organizations that interest you, etc. Money is not everything and for some, it may not be a huge proponent of your life's goals and dreams. However, money is a part of your life and you need it to some degree to reach your goals. So begin there—determine your monthly numbers in order to reach your goal. Will you need $10,000 per month or a million? Do you just want to travel the world and get by financially, creating as many relationships as possible with a diverse group of people, or do you want to build a major corporation? Personally, I want to build that orphanage in Africa. My desire is to help that group of people and that will require a lot of money. This goal requires me to map out not only the costs of building the orphanage but also of sustaining it. So, map out your goals, know your numbers, and do not go in blindly. Starting today, begin lining up your financial goals with your passions and what you want out of life.

Should you be writing down your goals regularly? Absolutely. In fact, I tell people to get into the habit of writing them down daily, when they wake up in the morning and before they go to bed at night. Just the act of writing it down on paper will be a huge step for some people. Once you begin writing them down, you start working out the steps, how long it will take to reach them, how much you will need to sacrifice to come up with the money, and so on. This daily habit will get you moving quicker than just keeping a mental list of things you hope to achieve one day. Start charting your journey and attaching numbers to it and I believe you have a much greater probability of being successful in bringing your vision to fruition.

WHO WILL YOU BECOME?

The fact that you chose to read this book over a fictional book or magazine is a huge step forward in being successful. It shows a willingness to commit three to four hours to learn new ways to achieve your dreams, whether it is through the Venn diagram, the business tips, action steps, etc. Taking the time to invest in yourself is a major indicator that you are the type of person who has the entrepreneurial spirit, drive, passion, and willingness to sacrifice now in the short term in order to reap rewards in the long term.

The person who reads this book cares about their future and the future of their family. They want to solve problems, whether that be creating a solution for world hunger or building a path for their family to get out of poverty. If this sounds like you, I want to commend you for your desire to create something extraordinary, to step outside of societal norms and chase after your dreams. It has been said that goals are the fuel in the furnace of achievement. As we pursue more and more dreams and make our goals bigger, we are essentially stoking the fire of our achievement.

That is what this book is all about—goals, dreaming big, and putting actionable steps in place to achieve whatever dream is in front of you. Whether you want to break free from generations of poverty, escape the 9–5, or finally reach financial freedom, my hope is to have offered you tangible solutions to clearly define your passion and take the first step of your journey. The mission behind this book is to wake people up to the reality that they can push beyond a polarizing economy, push the envelope and their dreams, and be the ones who challenge the status quo and break out of the middle class.

The truth is, our generation is lacking a leader; perhaps you will be the candidate to influence the Millennial generation, whether it be in business or politics. Are you up for the challenge? Will you be the front-runner who can help our generation overcome all of the problems and opposition it is facing? Let's stop using the vehicles of the past to achieve today's goals. The slate before you is blank—you don't have to color in the lines drawn by someone else; you have the power to design your own future.

Bonus Chapter—12

● ● ●

BOOTCAMP BUSINESS TIPS

How to make your business more sellable:

1. Independence—not owner-centric. If one person, client, etc. was taken away, the business would collapse.
2. Owners manual—turnkey. Explain systems for hiring, marketing, website design, billing, estimating, etc. Automate systems and record how everything works in the business. Include 1-, 3-, 5-year projections and details on how to hit sales numbers, grow, etc. Take the guesswork and trust out of the kind of buyer.
3. Learn more—**Listen to Podcast Episode 79**

Customer Lifetime Value Exn: (length of time), (contribution margin), (acquisition costs)
Length of time: 1/churn rate %
Contribution margin: revenue-costs
Acquisition costs: marketing dollars/ units sold
Learn more—**Listen to Podcast Episode 80**

If you offer a service business to residential clients, keep a credit card on file in case you have trouble getting payment from a client after 30 days. Stripe.com is recommended because they only require a card number and expiration date. This provider encrypts data and stores card information.

Learn more—**Listen to Podcast Episode 81**

The Positioning Statement template:

This is not a mission statement. You can fill in the blanks for every promotion, advertisement, and commercial you see. This can also be used in your own marketing strategy. This will help you define who you are targeting and what your USP (Unique Selling Proposition) is.

This statement will help *position* your brand in the market.

To _____ target market and need _____ our _____ brand _____ is _____ FOR _____ that _____ POD _____ because _____ RTB _____

* Target market and need: The *specific* audience you are trying to reach.
* Brand: This is just the name of your brand or product.
* FOR = Frame of Reference. What is the market? What is the industry/segment that the brand is competing in?
* POD = Points of Difference. What makes the brand/product special or unique?
* RTB = Reasons to Believe. How does the advertisement/marketing piece try to convince people to believe that the brand is the best and is different than everyone else?

Example: A positioning template for Gillette. Most Gillette ads show engineers and precision of blade technology, such as how sharp they are and the labs in which they were designed. For this type of advertisement, this may be the positioning statement:

To _____ athletic males between the ages of 25 and 40 _____ our _____ Gillette Fusion _____ is _____ facial shavers _____ that _____ gives the closest, smooth- est shave _____ because _____ our stud engineers make boss blade technology _____

Learn more—**Listen to Podcast Episode 78**

Analyze your website and its efficiency. Website.grader.com from HubSpot grades SEO and organization of website.

Google promotes companies that use their products. Use AdWords and create a Google Plus account. This is big, especially on mobile devices. Google Plus profiles are above the general search. Make sure all your reviews are posted on Google Plus. One of the fastest ways to get high in Google is through G+ reviews.

For companies that are geographically confined/local services, make sure that in your site title, header, footer and in keywords, you have ZIP codes and city names of the service area you cover. Google and Siri take the location of a mobile user very seriously and will show what is "closest" to them. Make sure you make it clear to search engines where you are.
Learn more—See BusinessBootcampPodcast.com

Cold calling is purely a numbers game. It isn't dead, unless you make it.

If 100 calls = 1 prospect and 3 prospects = 1 customer and 1 customer = $1000 (customer lifetime value), you need to call 300 people to attain 1 customer. You make $3.3 per cold call.

To make $1,000,000/hr, you need to call 300,000 people.

Need affordable design services? Use freelancer.com for initial logo designs. Use 99designs.com for larger projects once you get established. Toptal.com is great for long term developer and programmer hiring (Example: web design, book covers, etc.)

SEO Tips

Create a blog on your website for keywords—make sure it provides value to customers and isn't strictly commercial. Create how-to posts and show interesting facts about your industry.

Create some YouTube videos with links to your website. Post them on social media and your website.

Make sure Yelp and other review sites have a profile for your company, and that you are on Google places, Apple maps. Create some articles on article databases that point back with links to your site. Learn more—**Listen to Podcast Episode 63**

Is this a Good Real Estate Deal?

3 Quick Tips: Reference for Evaluating a Deal (Refer to the BiggerPockets podcast for more info)

--- If you are bent on buying a SFR (single family residence), at the very minimum, ask if you can cover your mortgage and taxes by renting it out. Use Rentometer.com to determine average rents in your area.

--- 1% rule and 2% rule: What percentage of the total mortgage loan does the monthly rent cover> For example, on a $200,000 property the rents must equal $2000/month to meet the 1% rule. Some investors say that the 1% is an absolute minimum and if the property meets the 2% rule, it more than likely the property will cash flow positively. This varies by market and demographic as well as what type and price of property you are investing in.

--- 50% rule: This rule takes into account that 50% of rent is usually eaten up by operating costs and vacancy. Thus, when using this rule, you should make sure the mortgage accounts for less than 50% of the rent cost. Thus, 50% for mortgage (capital expense) and 50% for operating costs and misc. If you can beat the 50% rule, you theoretically will cash flow positively on the property.

Made in the USA
Columbia, SC
30 July 2021